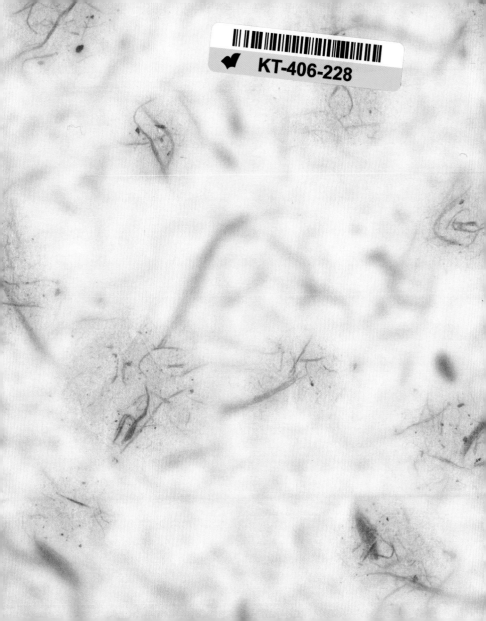

KT-406-228

To

_____

On the Occasion of

_____

From

_____

THE
DEEP PLACE
Where Nobody Goes

THE
DEEP PLACE
Where Nobody Goes

*Conversations with God on the
steps of my soul*

JILL BRISCOE

MONARCH
BOOKS

Oxford, UK & Grand Rapids, Michigan

Published in association with the literary agency of Alive Communications, Inc.,
7680 Goddard Street, Suite 2000, Colorado Springs, CO 80920, USA

Published by Monarch Books
an imprint of
Lion Hudson plc
Wilkinson House, Jordan Hill Road, Oxford, OX2 8DR.
Tel: +44 (0) 1865 302750   Fax: +44 (0) 1865 302757
Email: monarch@lionhudson.com   www.lionhudson.com/monarch

ISBN: 978 1 85424 683 7 (UK)
ISBN: 978 0 8254 6083 8 (USA)

First edition 2005.

Unless otherwise stated, Scripture quotations are taken from the Holy Bible, New
International Version © 1973, 1978, 1984 by the International Bible Society. Used by
permission of Hodder and Stoughton Ltd. All rights reserved. All remaining quotations
are taken from the Authorised (King James) Version of the Bible, published by
HarperCollins Publishers. Used by permission. All rights reserved.

A catalogue record for this book is available from the British Library.

Photos by: Bill Bain, Roger Chouler, Alison Hickey, Geoff Nobes, Jonathan Roberts, Anne Rogers,
Lion Hudson/David Townsend.

Printed in and bound in China, August 2012, LH17.

TO OUR TREASURED CHILDREN,
DAVID, JUDY AND PETE,
BY WHOM I AM MOST MARVELLOUSLY LOVED,
AND TO WHOM I OWE A DEBT OF
THANKFULNESS I SHALL NEVER BE ABLE TO
PAY. THANK YOU FOR LETTING ME LIVE IN THE
MATRIX OF THAT "MOTHER-HOLE" IN YOUR
HEARTS. THANK YOU FOR GIVING US OUR
GRANDCHILDREN, WHO LIGHT UP OUR LIVES
WITH JOY, EVERY ONE OF THEM.
AND ALL THIS BECAUSE OF HIM WHO MADE
OUR MOMENTS AND COUNTED OUT OUR
DAYS,
THIS GOD WE ALL LOVE AND SERVE, WHO HAS
GIFTED US WITH THE RARE REALITY OF ONE
OF REDEMPTION'S RICHEST REWARDS – A
REGENERATE FAMILY!

CONTENTS

COMMENDATION

*I*N THE PRECIOUS FAMILY OF GOD, Jill Briscoe has been my big sister for over thirty years…

The example of Jill's life…

The tenderness of Jill's heart…

The sensitivity of Jill's spirit…

The words of Jill's pen…

…all make me want to follow her to God's Front Door and enter into The Deep Place Where Nobody Goes. This little volume is like tonic to my weary prayer life. Drink deeply…and come alive to Him!

Anne Graham Lotz

PREFACE
MY HEARTBEAT

"GOD CAN TESTIFY THAT I LONG FOR ALL OF YOU WITH THE
AFFECTION OF CHRIST JESUS. AND THIS IS MY PRAYER: THAT
YOUR LOVE MAY ABOUND MORE AND MORE… "
Philippians 1:8–9

ᏩᎤ

I CARRY THEM WITH ME to the Deep Place where nobody goes. Those I love better than myself, gifts of grace so precious. I take my deep longings and hopes for my life and theirs to Him. He never disappoints me, but is ever there, waiting.

"Today I am so, so thankful. Can you hear it, Lover of my soul?"

"I hear it."

"It's my heartbeat."

"I know it well – I hear its language; I read its longing; I shape the love beats into prayers. The angels gather every one so none is lost – you are heard. Tell me, though I know already, who does your heart beat for today?"

"My heart beats for the man in my life! The one you gave me nearly 50 'man years' ago. My husband; my other self; my friend – for whom I thank You every day. How could You match me a man so well? One who never allows me to take myself too seriously? One who has brought the soft colours of life, love and laughter to my 'worry world', teasing out the knots of knottiness in my stomach – chivvying me into rest.

"One who constantly challenges me to be the woman You want me to be, because he insists on being the man You want him to be and nothing else! Jesus first and last: Jesus all in all! I LOVE that in him, perhaps above all else. What a gift! No grey in this partnership, only the rainbow of promises, even after rain. Hear me for this man of mine – and Yours."

"I hear you; it is recorded. I will bless him."

"Hear my heart beat for our adult children and their spouses: heart partners all in Jesus, loving and glory giving. Grow gold relationships like sunflowers, ever bright and beautiful in the garden of our small shared moments – and make me the perfect grandmother – even as you made me the perfect mother! (I wish!)

"I hear it; it is recorded. You didn't do it 'all' wrong, Jill! I will bless them all."

"And the grandchildren, what can I say…? How can You be so generous in gifting us with thirteen lives – each unique and precious – joy of our hearts. See them, Lord, I bring them all to the Deep Place for You to bless. Lay Your hands on their heads – fulfil our dreams for them. This is my heartbeat."

"I see them; I bless them."

"Above all, my God and King, hear my heart beat for *You*!

You who know me better than I could ever know myself. You see my poor heart seeking to enlarge its boundaries to better love the world you love. Help me to beat my heart into submission whenever it becomes hard or lukewarm, so it learns to die a little bit with sorrow when people need You, Lord, and there's no one to tell them. Send me, spend me, defend me.

"Hear, oh hear my heartbeat."

"I hear it: it is recorded. I will bless you now."

"Most of all, I want my words – the words in this little book – to matter to the ones who have faint hearts. Yet I know that for words of wisdom to make a difference, they have to come out of wise people and there is no short cut. I must stay long with You in the cool Deep Place where nobody goes – on the steps of my soul, by the Throne Room outside the Front Door – with the ever-wise God. In Your presence, on my face, and at Your feet I will know the words to use. Touch my mouth."

"It is done; it is recorded."

I was humbled greatly. He wrote every heartbeat down. Not one was lost.

So I left His side and climbed the stairs to the world at war with the Lamb, knowing the best thing I can do for those I love is to work at wisdom, fearing God, and laughing at the devil: working my head off to see His Kingdom come. I want to live for His honour, His smile, His people, and His kingdom work, *because I love* Him. This is my heartbeat!

TAKE A PEN AND PAPER...

TRY TAKING A PEN AND PAPER to the Deep Place where nobody goes. Then you can read His letters in the Golden Book and write a reply.

> I write it out on paper and I
>   think my thoughts out loud
> I speak my heart's foreboding and I pray about
>   the cloud
> Of deep and dark depression and a sense of dread and
>   doubt
> So I write it out on paper and I get my feelings out.
>
> Then I take it to the Throne Room and leave it there
>   above
> And I know that I am understood with sympathy and
>   love
> I wait a while in silence till the Spirit meets me there
> And He takes my piece of paper and He turns it into
>   prayer.

I bring my tired believing and my faith that pants for
    power
And I lay it at the altar in this quiet, sacred hour
And I ask for fire igniting weary faith and dying hope
And I cry for stern believing and I seek for power to
    cope

Then I read the treasured Scripture that will lift my
    spirits high
Turn tears to precious laughter and kiss my fears goodbye
I wait until He calms me down and nerves me for the
    fight
And then He leads me upwards and onwards in the
    night.

So I revel in these moments in the shadow of the Throne
Where I hear the Father's voice like many waters falling
    down
There's freedom and forgiveness and unremitting love
So I hate to leave the Throne Room for the shallow
    place above!

Sleeping forgiven, waking to grace
Nightmares forgotten, things back in place
Coming close to His footstool in the Throne Room
    above
He settles my soul, and I listen to love.

THE GRACE PLACE

"THEY THAT WAIT UPON THE LORD SHALL RENEW THEIR
STRENGTH; THEY SHALL MOUNT UP WITH WINGS AS EAGLES;
THEY SHALL RUN, AND NOT BE WEARY; AND THEY SHALL WALK,
AND NOT FAINT."

Isaiah 40:31 (Authorised Version)

───── ⟲ ─────

I RAN TO THE DEEP PLACE where nobody goes and found
Him waiting there.

"Where have you been?" He asked me.

"I've been in the shallow places where everyone lives," I
replied. I knew He knew. He just wanted me to admit I'd been
too busy being busy.

"I'm running out… " I began.

"Of course," he said. "I haven't seen you in a while."

He sat down on the steps of my soul in the Deep Place
where nobody goes and smiled at me. Angels sang; a shaft of light
chased away the shadows and brightened my daily day. I smiled
back.

"I'm such a fool… "

"Shhh," He said, putting His finger on my lips. He touched
my hurried heart. Startled, it took a deep breath and skidded to

a near stop. My spirit nestled into nearness in the Deep Place where nobody goes.

My soul spoke, then: He answered with words beyond music. Where "on earth" had I been while "heaven" waited? Such grace!

Lord, may all who turn these pages, and join me on the steps of my soul, discover this book to be a "Grace Place"!
Amen

The grace place

FLYING

GOING UP AND DOWN

"He was taken up before their very eyes,
and a cloud hid Him from their sight."
Acts 1:9

I HATE CLIMBING THROUGH cumulus clouds in an aeroplane. The frightening lurches of the aircraft still have the power to make me lean against Stuart (if he is with me), and grip his arm really tight. Even after all these years of flying I still look anxiously at the sky as we board a plane.

"Don't hang on to me," my husband says, grinning, "I'm going up and down too!" It's true, but I need some reassurance. Men are always so logical; but you know sometimes "logical" doesn't help! Now, here I was again, taking one more flight on a cloudy stormy day.

"I hate cumulus clouds," I muttered.

"Pretty," was His cryptic comment. He was looking out of the window, smiling.

"Oh, I'm sorry Lord, I didn't see You there. Yes, indeed they are very pretty." I didn't want to hurt His feelings, but when a small plane such as the one I was travelling in gets among those puffy white things, it's scary!

"Are you sure this aeroplane is safe, Lord?" I asked anxiously, as we hit an air pocket and dropped too many feet before levelling off.

He didn't answer, which made me a little nervous. Did He know something I didn't? Well, that was a silly thought! I knew He even knew my anxious thoughts, but I wondered if He really understood how hard it was being human and being hurtled through the clouds, even protected inside a machine. After all, He never had aeroplanes when He was on earth!

"I did it without one," He remarked, tracking my thoughts.

"Without what?" I asked startled.

"Without an aeroplane," He said.

"Oh! So you did!" We were quiet as I thought about that, and I remembered how He had ascended into heaven with all the disciples standing around watching Him!

"Was it bumpy going up?" I asked, hoping I wasn't being irreverent. I was relieved when He laughed.

"Not bad," he said, "a bit like this. There usually weren't many clouds around Galilee – unless a squall blew up suddenly." Then, "Remember what I said to my disciples just before I left them that day?"

"Yes, Lord, You said, 'Go into all the world and make disciples… and I am with you *always*.' That was a funny thing to say, when you were just about to disappear!"

"Some of my disciples were a little confused too – they doubted."

I knew He wanted me to believe He was with me "always" – even when I

wondered. I told Him I didn't want to doubt Him. I wanted to be like the disciples who believed. "Always," He had said, "always…". I sat back and thought about that as the plane continued on its bumpy way. "Always", like here and now, rising far above the earth through cumulus clouds. "Even to the end of the age."

"I'll remember that, Lord, next time I'm scared. When the clouds of fear hide You from sight, the bumps will remind me I don't want to doubt you."

"Good," He said. "Remember, I'm going up and down too! You can lean on me and grip my mighty arm!" After that I did, and guess what? I found out it was gripping me!

Lord, I love it that You "go up and down"

in the aeroplane with me! What an

incredible thing it is that we have such

marvellous ways of "Going into all the

world to preach the gospel". We really have

no excuse not to reach out to the ends of

the earth! Thank you that I live in this

wonderful age of technology.

Amen

THE WISH WAND

⁖

T WAS ON ONE MORE PLANE, going to one more place. I
had been asked to address a ton of teenagers on the subject "Do
Modern Christians Really Believe in Hell?" I was not looking
forward to it.

The man sitting next to me seemed to be, as someone said
rather cynically, "A self-made man who worshipped his creator!"

"But he seems to be a nice man," I commented to the Lord
somewhat defensively. "A good man – as men go!"

He who had been helping me to write a poem didn't reply,
just settled down to hear me out.

"As far as my brief hour's conversation with him has taken
me, Lord, he seems to be a good enough man!" I repeated. "He
goes to church quite often, and gives to charity. He thinks he's
good enough to get to heaven on his own merits, though."

"There is none good but God," He said. (That sounded
familiar.)

Suddenly my companion in the next seat asked me what I was studying.

"I'm reading about heaven and hell," I answered.

"How interesting," he replied. I had rather hoped he would hastily hide behind his newspaper, embarrassed at the eccentric woman he had had the misfortune to sit beside. "Why would you be reading about that?" he asked. "Are you a nun?"

"Er, no," I muttered. "Well," I glanced at Him and He nodded encouragingly. "I believe in both," I said hurriedly.

"You believe in both?" he asked incredulously. "You mean in both heaven *and* hell?"

"Yes," I said firmly. The lady the other side of me promptly went to sleep!

"Well, I don't know anyone in our neighbourhood that believes in hell," my "nice man" said. "Heaven maybe − yes, definitely − but not hell! Not in this enlightened age."

I didn't answer. We fell silent and I hoped he had finished talking about it. I returned to my work. I had been composing a poem on hell.

"Why don't you share it with him," suggested the Lord.

I was struck dumb. "I couldn't, I mean − it's for teenagers."

"But they are mostly Christians, Jill. This poem could cause non-believers to question."

"But it's for kids," I said again stubbornly. "Not businessmen in sharp suits." I didn't look at Him, I knew what He was thinking.

Did I believe in hell? Really believe? Did I believe people of all ages wished away biblical truth? I knew the answer. I believed. And what was more I knew, however I sought to describe such a lost state for lost people I would never get close to the frightful reality of the godless who were "without Christ, without God, and without hope".

Suddenly my poem seemed very juvenile. Not at all clever – and heavy with fire and brimstone.

He who spoke more about hell than heaven when He was on earth asked me quietly, "Do you believe what you wrote?"

"Well, sort of!"

"Sort of?"

"Well, Lord, I'm using a bit of imagination, but I believe in the truth behind it, that there is a state where God is not – and that is hell. And I do believe that there are so many people, even nice people like this man in his nice suit who is living life on a wing and a prayer, taking their chances just wishing that there won't be such a reality." There was silence. The man was looking at me strangely.

"Will *you* tell him it's true Lord?" I asked desperately. "If you tell him he will listen."

"Yes," He answered. I was floored – and delighted. My heart leaped!

"Through you," He said. My heart dropped! I might have known it!

I took a deep breath, handed over my poem, and said, "I tried to imagine that I'd died and landed in hell with my wishes and nothing else." He took it readily enough and began to read.

I shut my eyes dashed to the Deep Place where nobody goes and threw myself at His feet. "Help – ."

He smiled, and sent me back to the shallow place where everyone lives, to wait on my friend till he had absorbed my so inadequate attempt to make people wonder if such dire reality existed.

I prayed all the time he read my poem. "Oh Lord, let him ask, 'Could it be true?' And if he should ask, tell him he shouldn't rely on wishes, but rather the WORD!" As his eyes followed the lines, I shut my eyes and repeated the poem to myself.

I had a little wish wand and I waved it to and fro
Whenever thoughts turned heavenward, or the other
    place you go.
I thought it safe to trust it with my whole eternal soul
So I wished the life I lived on earth would get me to
    my goal.

I wished that all would get to heaven, whatever they
    believed,
That Buddha sat at God's right hand, that New Age be
    received
I wished that Paul had changed his mind, that Jesus
    wasn't right

Because he spoke of lostness and a dark eternal
     night;
About the way to heaven, one truth,
     one narrow gate,
And I was so broadminded that I
     wished away my fate!

So I waved my little wish wand in
     the patient face of Him
Who met me at the gates of heaven and
     wouldn't let me in
I e-mailed heaven's congressman, but he courteously
     replied
That I should have left my wish wand at the feet of
     Him who died!

For wishes could not wish away a lifetime of rejection
And wishes could not dress my soul in heaven's own
     perfection
And wishes could not save me now for hell was so
     obscene
That wishes there die ghastly deaths, strangled with a
     scream

So I took my little wish wand into hell the day I died,
And I waved it at the serpent as he slithered to my side.

It was dark, but I could see him and all I knew was fear
And no matter how I waved my wand he wouldn't
    disappear

Oh, I wished that I had wished aright, I wished I lived
    again
And I wished I had a body that was not racked with
    pain
I wished I could remember something other than the
    dirt
I wished I could forget my sin as every memory hurt.
Oh I wished and wished and wished, that I could have
    another chance
To cast upon the crucified one saving trusting glance –

But the devil took my wish wand and he laughed
    right in my face
And I went to live eternally in darkness and disgrace
I never wished a wish again; I had no heart to try
For hell is where hope ended and where all my wishes
    died!

The plane was landing and my new friend and I began to talk
about the danger of wishing away eternal truth.

"Do you know the verse, 'God so loved the world that He

gave His one and only Son, that whoever believes in Him will not perish but have everlasting life'? " I asked him.

"Of course," he said. "I go to church, but I thought that was enough. I've just never applied John 3:16 to me or to my wishes!"

It seemed to me – I heard the words quite clearly as if a thousand of God's angels were shouting it, "THEREFORE CHOOSE LIFE!"

I added my voice to their witness, and prayed for him. He was such a nice man. A good man who needed the Lord! Just a man in a nice suit who wasn't aware he was dancing with death – the eternal sort – and needed to be alerted to a very real and present danger.

*Dear Lord, who came to save the good,
the bad and the indifferent,
enlighten the lost to their lostness, the confused to truth and the good to their need of a Saviour. Use me to tell them.*

Amen

HEART HUNGRY

"THE WIFE OF A MAN FROM THE COMPANY OF THE PROPHETS,
CRIED OUT TO ELISHA, 'YOUR SERVANT MY HUSBAND IS DEAD,
AND YOU KNOW THAT HE REVERED THE LORD. BUT NOW HIS
CREDITOR IS COMING TO TAKE MY TWO BOYS AS HIS SLAVES.' "

2 Kings 4:1

HAVE YOU EVER FELT "HUNGRY" for your children? Did you lose your grandchildren through divorce? Have your relationships been severed by misunderstanding? Did you have to move to another city, or even another country and leave someone you love behind? Then you will understand what it means to be "heart hungry".

"I miss them all so much, Lord."

"I know."

I was at the other end of the earth, or so it seemed, travelling on my own, high in the sky over rough inhospitable terrain. I was thousands of miles away from my family and friends. I turned to Him who holds the whole world in His hands.

Suddenly, I had an insatiable desire to feel my grandchildren's arms around me, and their kisses on my cheek. It was a familiar hunger pang. "It's like a deep want that can't be satisfied, Lord. Yes,

I'm heart hungry for my grandkids. Most of all, I miss their kisses – you know, when I lean down within striking distance like my mother used to do, and pat my cheek and demand, 'Kiss me here.' "

"It's good."

"Good?"

"Yes, it means you all love each other very much. If you didn't you wouldn't feel it so deeply." I looked at him a little dubiously. He smiled. (I love it when He does that. I never want Him to stop.)

"But it will be months before I see them again!"

"Yes." He reminded me about 2 Kings 4:1–6 and I fished out my Bible from my flight bag and reread it.

It was all about a young widow who lost everything that makes life worth living. They were attending Elisha's Bible school at the time. Her husband died, and she had so many debts she had to sell everything to pay the bills. So she cried out to Elisha that the creditor was on the way to take away her children as collateral.

"How awful," I said to the Lord. "To lose a husband, and then to lose all your kids!" I ruminated that not a few women I knew, who had been left by their husbands and who were fighting custody battles, understood a little of her pain.

Somehow it all reminded me of my mother when Stuart and I left for America. She was a new widow and I had to tell her we were emigrating to the USA, taking her three grandchildren far away, just when she needed us the most! The ride with the children to her home in Liverpool to tell her was one of the worst and longest days of my life! Knowing she had a phobia about flying and that she would never come to see us didn't help.

At the end of that dark day, as we said goodbye, I remembered her bending over David, Judy and Pete, tapping her cheek with her finger as her habit was. "Kiss me here," she demanded, tears coursing down her face. They lifted their little faces up in love and obeyed. They looked a little frightened and very sad. I was a basket case. My poor mum. She had lost a husband, and now she was losing me – and her grandchildren. What in the world would she do without their kisses?

The incident had birthed a poem at that time, and I scribbled it out again now in my prayer diary.

> As feather is to bird on high
> Or rain is to a cloud,
> As light to angel wings in heaven
> As laughter, laughter laughed out loud,
> As leaf to tree and leg to knee
> As clear brook to the hart,
> Are children to the widow,
> And kisses to her heart.
>
> As sunshine to the winter earth,
> As frogs are to a pond,
> As shooting star to galaxy
> As planet to beyond

As kitten to a dish of milk
And horse to rope and cart,
Are children to the widow,
And kisses to her heart.

As baby is to Mother's breast
And hearth to wandering man,
Foundations to a building
And pancakes to a pan;
As hairspray is to hair and curl
And dartboard is to dart,
Are children to the widow
And kisses to her heart.

I remembered how, on the lengthy ride home from my mother's house, I cried for a long time, trying to do it quietly for the kids' sake (they were sitting in the back seat). I wanted to run back and pack up my beloved mother in a parcel and bring her with us. I wondered how long it would be before the children or I would give her our kisses again. These were hard memories!

As we left England on that dreary November day in 1970, I looked at Stuart beside me; he was sleeping. I looked at the kids, and they were playing. I looked up as a shadow passed my seat, and found Him there.

I didn't know I had any more tears left but I cried more! "Kiss me here," I whispered, tapping my cheek with my finger.

He bent down and I felt the breath of God brush my heart. It felt like the kiss of heaven. But then, that is exactly what it was. Seldom have I needed Him more than at that moment.

"Don't worry about your mother," He said softly. "When you can't, I can." I knew He was talking about the kisses. He moved on then, and I thought about the heart hunger that we poor creatures suffer as we are separated for whatever reason from those we love. I finished my poem.

> As breath of God upon my heart
> When I am far away,
> As Gilead's soothing balm that heals
> My homesickness this day,
> As worry for the ones I leave
> Behind me all alone
> Melts into trust in You who reign
> On high upon Your throne.
>
> So all I need to do is walk
> Into the pattern planned,
> And trust the ones I love so much
> Into Your nail-pierced hands.
> I'll go for gold and live for You
> And try to do my part:
> And this will bring me comfort and
> Your kisses to my heart!

I looked around, jerked from my memories of nearly 35 years ago by the announcement in a strange language that we were landing soon. This time, all these years later, I was the one who was all alone: feeling like the widow in the familiar story, and needing some little arms around my neck and some kisses on my cheek.

So I went to the Deep Place where nobody goes, and felt the breath of God on my soul all over again. It was enough.

"I am the same yesterday, today and for ever," He said, close at hand.

"I know it, Lord."

"When you can't, I can." I heard Him say, yet one more time.

"Do it again, Lord. Do it for them – for me!"

I believe, far away across a few oceans, the sleeping children felt the breath of God!

Lord when we get hungry for those we love

so very much, comfort us.

Kiss us better with the breath of your Spirit.

Mend our hungry, hurting hearts.

Amen

ON BEING AN EXAMPLE

"GIVE THANKS IN ALL CIRCUMSTANCES,
FOR THIS IS GOD'S WILL FOR YOU."
1 Thessalonians 5:18

❧

WAS BACK IN THE USA after a horrendous journey home from the heartland of Russia. I was attempting to meet Stuart in Canada for a big convention, relieved to think that I would have a good night's sleep at home before travelling again. Russia had done me proud, delivering me safely and on time to Chicago, but then the nightmare began! Suffice it to say, after over 24 hours in the air and many more at airports, I found my flights cancelled and I couldn't get home to sleep and pick up clean clothes.

Somehow, I ended up in an airport hotel at midnight, due to return to Chicago to get my Canadian flight only three hours later! I could hardly get up when the too-cheerful night clerk rang my room. I made my way back to the airport in the dark to find I was on standby for a plane that had been cancelled for technical reasons. (I fought a desire to walk over on the tarmac and kick the wheels!)

Would I get to Canada? I worried. I was due to start speaking that night. Feeling very sorry for myself, I looked for the first person I could find on whom to vent my frustration. Then, seeing the long queue in front of me trying to rebook, I decided to call the airline on my mobile phone to sort out a new itinerary by myself. After talking to endless machines, I eventually got a real live person on the end of my phone....

She answered me with a bright, "Yes, can I help you?" Wonderful, here I go! I thought.

"My name is Jill Briscoe," I began, "I am a frequent flyer on your airline and I am just about... "

"Yes Ms Briscoe? Oh, Ms Briscoe? You're not the lady who writes Christian books, are you?" I had opened my mouth to blast the poor woman at the other end of the line about the wretched treatment I had encountered. Then she said again, "Jill Briscoe! I think you're a wonderful Christian lady. I've heard you speak." Bother, now I couldn't complain.

I hung up, muttering, "Thanks, I'll figure this out myself." Which I did, after an hour's work.

On checking in to my new flight, the man behind the desk noticed a logo on my coat. I literally had my mouth open to tell him off (even though the whole mess had nothing to do with him), when he pointed to the logo.

"Are you a Christian?" he asked loudly.

Foiled again!

As I went through security the tired nightshift worker put a red line through my ticket and said, "You've been selected for extra screening! Did he say screening or screaming? I wondered.

I began to strip off my clothes and was just about to snap, "Look at me, do I fit the profile? I am a grandmother of thirteen," when the girl going through my luggage found my Bible and put it out on the table for all to see! Somehow I kept my mouth shut.

My next chance to let fly was after my new flight *and* the one after that were cancelled! Did I have the strength to make it back to the check-in counter again that day, never mind to Canada? In the long queue of equally frustrated passengers there was nothing to do but talk as we waited impatiently for everyone to be rerouted once more.

A fellow passenger in front of me looked a perfect person to vent on. I struck up a conversation, eager to share the details of my horrendous journey, when this total stranger started to pour out her heart to me. She was in really big trouble and maybe she mistook my stunned face for a sympathetic one. Anyway, as I listened to her, what could I do but talk about Jesus?

"What is this, a conspiracy?" I almost shouted at the Lord. He had suddenly appeared in the queue in front of me. I noticed He looked cheerful and patient. All right for Him, I dared to think (quickly in case he heard my thoughts). It wasn't really fair – he didn't need luggage and His clothes always seemed fresh and white! He was always up on His sleep too.

I wondered where He was heading and I noticed He didn't have any bags. That's good – they'd only lose them for Him if He did, I thought!

He turned around and showed me a cartoon in the paper He

was reading. It showed a man at the check-in counter telling the desk clerk, "I'd like to go somewhere near my luggage." He smiled; I didn't!

"Lord, I'm so glad you're here," I began, "can I whine to you? I've been trying for days, so it seems, to find someone – "

He asked, "Why should I have to listen? And why do you think it's all right to whine to me?"

"I don't need to be an example to You," I explained.

"Is this hardship or inconvenience?" He asked me suddenly.

"Inconvenience," I replied subdued.

"Right. Think about our Russian friends and all you've seen and heard from them about real hardship. Think about their lives and how they live with frustrating things all day, every day. Did you hear *them* whine? Don't get all worked up about inconvenience. Learn patience in the face of frustration: give thanks in all things!"

I eventually arrived in Canada in time for a restorative seven hours' sleep before the work began. Four days later Stuart and I returned home. Stuart told me to get into the waiting car while he got the luggage. He was gone too long.... At last, he appeared with his suitcase, but someone else had taken mine by mistake! Well, at least I could whinge to Stuart.

Why should I tire him out with my complaints? I thought, just in time. He had had an even worse time than me getting to Canada.

Then I remembered a verse in the Golden Book: "When I complained, my spirit was overwhelmed."

I decided to try being thankful. After all, I had a lot to be thankful about.

Lord, forgive my capacity for giving in too easily to frustration.

I'm sorry. Help me to "give thanks in all things".

Amen

THE DEEP PLACE WHERE NOBODY GOES

HUMILITY

THE STEPS OF MY SOUL

"LET THOSE WHO BOAST, BOAST IN THE LORD."
1 Corinthians 1:31

⟨❧⟩

*I*F SOMEONE WAS WRITING A BOOK about you what would they say? If you were writing your own book about yourself, what would you say? And how would you handle the attention if it did well in the market place? Would it be all about Him, or all about you?

My new book was hot off the press at a large convention. A long queue of people had lined up to have me sign it, and a girl had just bought ten of them! "These are for all the most important people in my life," she said gratefully. I tried to look suitably *un*pleased about her good judgement in purchasing my work, but my ego was grinning from ear to ear!

"Jill," I heard His unmistakable voice from the Deep Place inside me, where nobody goes. "We need to talk." I went at once to the steps of my soul and found Him patiently waiting there.

One thing I love about the Deep Place is the fact that I can

go right on doing what I'm doing and sit on the steps of my soul at the same time!

"You know," He said, "When you come through the Front Door one day, and you ask me, 'Lord, did you read my book?' I am going to reply, 'No. Did you read Mine?'"

I was shocked.

"Lord, I'm sorry," then less than truthfully, "I hate my proud spirit."

"Hate it enough to be done with it then," He replied rather sternly.

"Maybe I'd better not do any more signings at meetings," I said contritely, trusting He wouldn't notice – I hoped He wouldn't take me up on it. He noticed!

"That wouldn't hurt for a while," He said. "Take a time out on the steps."

"Like… like… a real 'time out'?" I asked with a vision of my grandkids being sent to sit on the stairs after a misdemeanour! "For how long?"

"Until you can handle this little bit of limelight I trusted you with." Then I understood He meant "those steps" – the steps of my soul! Obediently, I mentally sat still just where I was in the Deep Place where nobody goes, while continuing to sign away in the shallow places where everyone lives.

"Tell me when time's up, Lord," I said (just like my grandkids). I found it quite impossible to sit where I was in the Deep Place with Him and still be proud.

"My pleasure," He replied. He kept me there till the queue was cleared and I returned to the airport where nobody knew me at all! Actually, that felt a whole lot better than being in the limelight.

Later that night, as I was drifting off to sleep, I made a mental list of how to help myself in such circumstances.

1. A time of prayer just before the signings would help.
2. I would ask one of my prayer partners to pray that God would keep me humble (though I would ask her not to pray "too hard!").
3. I would memorize a "humility" verse or two. For example: "Humble yourselves, therefore, under God's almighty hand… " or
   "He made Himself nothing, taking the very nature of a servant."
4. I wouldn't sign any books!
5. Wherever else I sat, I would sit on the steps of my soul at the same time!

Nearly asleep, I heard the Front Door open. The choir was practising – the hymn was wonderfully familiar – one of my favourites:

> Forbid it, Lord, that I should boast,
> Save in the death of Christ, my God,
> All the vain things that charm me most,
> I sacrifice them to His blood.

I knew they were singing it for me! I sang it too, until I slept, forgiven, ready for the challenge of keeping humble on the morrow!

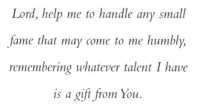

Lord, help me to handle any small
fame that may come to me humbly,
remembering whatever talent I have
is a gift from You.
Amen

A PRAYER FOR HUMILITY

*T*WO THOUSAND YEARS AGO, You came into Jerusalem in humility, Lord, just as You come into our world today.

You stooped to conquer then and You stoop to conquer now by visiting our little lives – our miniature moments.

Some people welcomed You then, and some people welcome You now, little realizing that accepting You as Saviour means accepting Your cross.

Because You came as a lowly King we can reign in life with You, but not without the cross.

Humility

The shadow of Your cross must mark us out of the generic pack; stamping us with integrity and acts of sacrificial love, mirroring Calvary.

May our selfless service say to a watching world: 'the cross is our abiding place'.

We pray for our churches dear Lord;
    For teachers teaching,
        preachers preaching,
            singers singing,
                prayers praying,
                    carers caring,
                        helpers helping!

May all know the impact of Your Spirit of humility, in their attitudes and actions bringing all under the scrutiny of the cross.

Cause us all to reassess our mindset, appropriate Your power and live daily unto You, Lord Jesus,
    In Your Spirit and for Your sake,
    Amen

ON BEING WELL KNOWN

"HUMBLE YOURSELVES BEFORE THE LORD,
AND HE WILL LIFT YOU UP."

James 4:10

◦

AVE YOU EVER BEEN SUDDENLY aware that you are
feeling proud, but unable to do anything about it? It can happen
anytime of the day or night. What do you do when that happens?
I go to the Deep Place where nobody goes!

I was being introduced at an important meeting. I had come
to talk about humility.

"Don't listen," He advised – He forbade anyone to "publish
His miracles" when He lived in the shallow places where everyone
lives. I jumped. I didn't realize He was sitting next to me on the
platform. I felt embarrassed. The conference was quite expensive!

"Make no charge for the gospel," He said in my ear.

"Oh, I remember, Paul said that!"

"I told him to," He responded mildly.

What was it now I wondered, as I struggled to remember
Paul's advice. "'What then is my reward? Just this: that in
preaching the gospel I may offer it free of charge, and so make
use of my rights in preaching it.'"

"Give them the cheque back," He suggested, in tune with my thoughts. "That's a lot of money from an organization like this." I pretended not to hear – anyway, I was looking over the first point in my notes. It was about sacrificial giving!

"Have you noticed, everyone offers to serve in a voluntary capacity these days, but expects to be paid for it?" He asked conversationally. "On the other hand, a workman is worthy of his hire." It was getting very hard to concentrate on my message when He kept talking to me all the time, but I could hardly ask Him to stop!

"Jill Briscoe is a well-known – "

"I said, don't listen," He said more loudly.

"OK."

"Don't believe your own press," He advised. "I can't use a smug person. Switch off. Anyway, what have you that you did not receive?"

"Nothing, Lord," I replied, honestly enough. "How can I help myself?"

"Pretend they are talking about someone else," He suggested.

"Like who?" I asked, interested.

"Like, someone you don't know whom you have come to hear." Well, that was a novel idea! He had achieved His purpose. By now my introductions were over and I realized He had succeeded in distracting me.

"Keep me humble, Lord," I prayed as I rose to speak.

"That should be easy enough," He replied cheerfully. "You've got a lot to be humble about!"

I can't remember too much about the talk I gave but I had to repeat it later, so between the two presentations, I went to the Deep Place where nobody goes, and spent time at His feet. Then I redid my notes. He said the talk came out quite differently. I think I heard Him say He liked it a lot better the second time around!

Lord, keep me humble of soul. Help me "not to think of myself more highly than I ought to think". Teach me to esteem others better than myself. Make me like you.

Amen

LEARN TO BE SMALL

〜

*H*AVE YOU EVER HEARD the Still Small Voice speaking really loudly? Funny. It's a paradox. You know: like "you give to get" or "you die to live". There it was again. It could not be ignored. I went to the Deep Place where nobody goes.

"Did you say something?" I asked Him.

"You know I said something."

"Er, was it 'Learn to be little'?"

"Do you have a problem with that, Jill?"

"Yes, because I want to be big!"

"That's honest enough!"

I sat down and read in the Golden Book about the Lord stepping down from heaven's glory. "That was a mighty step," I said in awe.

"Learn to step down," He said.

I knew then why He had said what He said. I was struggling with wanting to step up!

"Let this mind be in you that was also in Christ Jesus," I read.

Then I was lost in the wonderful hymn that sang a song about my wonderful Lord, and in my mind's eye I saw that great graph of grace – from heaven's glory to hell's halls – He had made for me.

"You laid it down," I murmured. "Image, Status, Glory, Honour, Control; all that the world (and my haughty heart) holds dear. You let it go. Your Father didn't have to prise your fingers open."

"Learn to be small," He said.

I thought about a quote I had heard. "Learn to do something great." I put it together. God was asking me to do something great: to learn to be small so that He could be big in my life. He was asking me to have the mind of Christ. "I don't know how to do it," I began awkwardly.

The Golden Book lay in my lap. The song sung by angels rang in my ears. "Lay it down… Lay it down… Lay it down." And then there was silence.

I climbed the steps of my soul and found the world in the shallow places where everyone lives, stepping up, fighting to be first, pushing to the front, sounding loud, rude and just being human. I joined them.

But all day long I heard the song of angels, who so long ago were left stunned, holding His glory in their hands, glory laid aside in the hallway of His home, waiting till Ascension Day.

The song wouldn't quit. I swear the choir was standing on the steps of my soul! He laid it all down. He came down, knelt down, was nailed down on a rough-hewn cross – it was all about "down". I knew then with a sharp pang that my life was usually all about "up"!

Christ Jesus:
Who, being in very nature God,
did not consider equality with God
something to be grasped,
but made himself nothing,
taking the very nature of a servant,
being made in human likeness.
And being found in appearance as a man,
He humbled Himself
and became obedient to death –
even death on a cross!
Therefore God exalted Him to the
highest place
and gave Him the name that is
above every name,
that at the name of Jesus every knee
should bow,
in heaven and on earth and under
the earth,
and every tongue confess that Jesus Christ is Lord,
to the glory of God the Father.

Philippians 2:6–11

"Do something great, learn to be small." The Voice wasn't loud any more – just insistent! "Your attitude should be the same as that of Christ Jesus: learn to be small; learn to be small; learn to be small!"

"Lord." (Oh it felt so good – just saying that word and meaning it!) "Lord, Lord – " and I joined in the high hymn of heaven with all my heart.

Can you hear it: the golden

hymn?

Shh! Listen to the angels.

What are you doing up on

your feet? You're too tall:

learn to be little!

Want to be great?
Then learn to be small
A lover of Jesus
And servant of all.

Want to be rich?
Then learn to be poor
Give Him your everything
Then give Him more.

Want to be happy?
Then learn to be sad
Weep with the weepnig
Visit the bad.

Want to be great?
Then learn to be small
A lover of Jesus
Servant of all.

FISHING

HAVE YOU EVER SEEN
A FISH JUMP?

"ASK AND IT WILL BE GIVEN TO YOU."
Matthew 7:7

THE SUN WAS SHINING but it was a dark day. Have you ever had one of those? When there is darkness inside, it doesn't seem to matter how bright the sun shines in the sky. We had the world praying, or so it seemed. One of our children was in trouble and so prayer was requested and promises were made. "We will pray," they said, and I knew they would, and were. Yet nothing had changed.

After a sleepless night, and as soon as the sun rose, I took a blanket, made myself a cup of tea, and went down to the side of the little fishing lake by our house in Wisconsin. It was just a step further to go to the Deep Place where nobody goes. I found Him waiting. Did our little lake remind Him of Galilee, I wondered?

"Hullo."

"Hullo."

"There are lots of people praying."

"I hear them."

"Then… " I couldn't go on.

He finished it for me, "… Why haven't you seen any answers?"

"Well – yes!"

Silence. I began to cry. Sitting there in those early morning hours I thought about our trouble. What did I believe? That God answered the prayers of His people? Yes, I believed that God indeed answered prayer. Then why had we seen no evidence of the fact?

Reading my thoughts, He drew my attention to the beauty of the lake. It was like glass, with myriad vapours in rainbow colours chasing across the surface. Isn't it funny how you can be looking at a beautiful thing and never see it, because all you can see is your trouble?

"Are there fish in there?" He asked me unexpectedly.

"Of course."

"How do you know?"

"Well, we've caught them, with the grandkids – remember?" He nodded. He loved it when we had the whole gang here, playing and fishing together. So did I!

"Do you believe that just below this glass-like surface, where nothing moves, there is life and activity?"

"Yes."

I looked at the smooth surface of our little lake and greatly wondered. What was He saying to me? Suddenly one of His fish jumped – such beautiful creatures, such variety. Then the words came clearly, "Do you have to see a fish jump to believe they are there, Jill?"

I knew at once where He was going with this! I thought about His question. He was asking me to trust Him. To believe that He was indeed hearing all the prayers from around the world on our behalf. The surface of the situation appeared smooth and still as far as I could see, just like the lake, but God was at work. Yes, He was – below the seemingly indifferent surface.

"Speak to me," He said.

It took a little while – as I wrestled with my hurt at His seeming neglect of our urgent prayers, but I knew He wanted me to stay there until I could say what needed to be said and mean it.

At last I said, as honestly as I was able, "I will believe You have this thing in hand, Lord, despite all seeming evidence to the contrary. Yes, hear me, Lord, I will believe." Then peace came, and a smile worked its way across my heart – that felt so good!

How was it, I asked myself, I had not noticed how brightly the warm sun was shining, and the myriad colours of the lake looked so beautiful?

Dear Lord, help us to believe you hear and answer prayer and that despite the stillness of the surface situation, You work in the hidden places in the power of your Spirit. No Lord, I do not need to see a fish jump or a prayer answered. I will believe.

Amen

MY FATHER WAS
A FISHERMAN

" 'COME, FOLLOW ME,' JESUS SAID,
'AND I WILL MAKE YOU FISHERS OF MEN.' "
Matthew 4:19

⬡

MY FATHER WAS A FISHERMAN, and I am my father's
daughter. When my sister and I were young, my father taught us
to make flies under a microscope to catch trout in the beautiful
Lake District – Wordsworth's country – or in Northern Ireland
where the mountains of Mourne sweep down to the sea. He was
a serious fisherman and he taught us his skills. He said to us,
"Follow me and I will make you 'Fishers of fish!' " So we
followed him because we loved him, and he taught us his trade.

Later, when I was a teenager, I found faith in Christ while in
hospital in Cambridge. The nurse who led me to the Lord gave
me a Bible and I read Matthew 4:19. My heart leaped with
instant recognition – it was simple! My Father was a fisherman
and I was my Father's daughter. I was to follow Him because I
loved Him and He would teach me His trade. He would make
me a "Fisher of men"!

So I pulled up my boat to the shore – left everything and followed Him.

This grand adventure – this laughing life has had its challenges! Pulling people out of a sea of confusion and landing them safely on eternity's shore is not for sissies. But I would have it no other way. I have learned that if I will but fish in deep waters, where He directs – for He alone knows where the fish are – my nets will break with blessings.

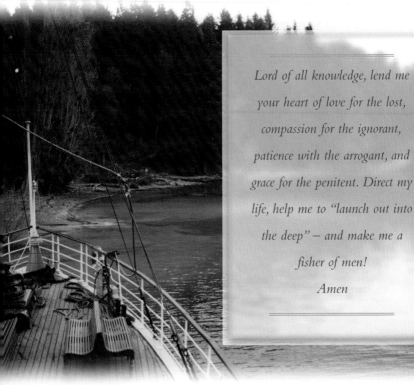

Lord of all knowledge, lend me your heart of love for the lost, compassion for the ignorant, patience with the arrogant, and grace for the penitent. Direct my life, help me to "launch out into the deep" – and make me a fisher of men!

Amen

PLAYING GAMES WITH JESUS

"THEY BEGAN TO CALL OUT TO HIM, 'HAIL, KING OF THE JEWS!'
AGAIN AND AGAIN THEY STRUCK HIM ON THE HEAD WITH A
STAFF AND SPAT ON HIM... AND WHEN THEY HAD MOCKED
HIM, THEY TOOK OFF THE PURPLE ROBE AND PUT HIS OWN
CLOTHES ON HIM. THEN THEY LED HIM OUT TO CRUCIFY HIM."

Mark 15:18–20

⁓

WE WERE IN THE HOLY LAND with a group from our church, in the days when it was safe to take people on tours. One night my husband said: "Jill, why don't you say something to the group tomorrow when we visit 'the Pavement'?" I looked at him dumbstruck. These pavement stones he spoke about were preserved deep down under a church. It was believed to be – with good reason – the very place, and the very pavement stones, where Jesus was scourged and mocked by the Roman soldiers before He was crucified.

What could I say? How could I even get the words out of

my mouth? I muttered that I would "think of something". That night, I went to the Deep Place where nobody goes and waited with some trepidation for Him.

"Hullo."

"Hullo."

"Um…". I didn't know where to begin. Without speaking, He handed me the Gospel of John, opened at chapter 19.

"Read verses 1–3," He said. "I did it for you!"

Then Pilate took Jesus and had Him flogged. The soldiers twisted together a crown of thorns and put it on His head. They clothed Him in a purple robe and went up to Him again and again, saying, "Hail, king of the Jews!"

And they struck Him in the face.

"Oh Lord, the men You made – they played games with You!"

"You have been in that place before. Remember, the stones have a game marked out on them."

I remembered the squares, and our guide explaining that the victim of this cruel sport would stand in the centre square and wherever the dice landed, the prisoner was subjected to the torture depicted on that particular stone.

"The dice fell on the scourge, mockery and the crown of thorns for me," He said quietly.

I didn't say a word, but laboured far into the night to capture as best I could my heart's response to the Pavement. I could hardly speak the next day, but as the group gathered round I knelt down on what to me is one of the most sacred places on the planet. The place where the human race dared to play games with Jesus. There I offered Him my thanks:

> Scourged my King, a plaited crown,
> Runs the blood of Godhead down?
> Ripped the flesh, the beard pulled out
> Cruel the sport and rude the shout.
> Scourged my King, a plaited crown,
> Runs the blood of Godhead down?

> Scourged my King in soldiers' den,
> Exposed to beasts who, dressed like men,
> Smelled the blood of prey soon caught
> Set my Jesus all at naught!
> Scourged my King, and fool of made,
> God in heaven, what price You paid –
> And all because of my heart's need:
> Sinful thoughts and sinful deeds,
> A dirty soul that dirtied Thee
> O'er bloodied earth on bloodied tree.
> `Scourged my King, a plaited crown,
> Runs the blood of Godhead down?

Scourged my King, a plaited crown –
Here I kneel a-trembling down,
Beat my fists in silent fury
While my world ignores your story;
Scourged my King, a plaited crown
Runs the blood of Godhead down?

Scourged my King, a plaited crown,
Runs the blood of Godhead down?
Can I doubt Your Father's loss?
Broken God on broken cross.
Do I bear wound or mark in me
That mirrors Thine on Calvary?
Scourged my King, a plaited crown
Runs the blood of Godhead down?

He was there – we all felt Him draw near – we heard His footsteps. We stayed silent, overwhelmed with a sense of loss, rage and gratitude all rolled up in one. Then the next group of pilgrims crowded us out, and our group moved on.

Lord, deliver us from ever taking You

lightly, from trivializing You, from

"playing games" with You.

Make us ever thankful.

Amen

BRUISED BUT NEVER BROKEN

"A BRUISED REED HE WILL NOT BREAK,
AND A SMOULDERING WICK HE WILL NOT SNUFF OUT."
Isaiah 42:3

⸺⸺⸺ ♋ ⸺⸺⸺

THE REED WAS USED TO PLAY MUSIC, or give service to the writer as a pen. The wick of the candle existed to give light to all in the house. But what happened if the reed was broken or the wick smothered?

Have you ever felt like a bruised reed? Or that someone has smothered the little flame of your life? Perhaps you are living in a difficult marriage, or you find yourself struggling with rebellious kids who have bruised you. Maybe church people have hurt you: smothered your enthusiasm and disappointed you. Inadvertently, you may have been the one who has done the bruising. Maybe you have deeply disappointed someone you love and they are bruised and broken because of your words and actions.

If you are in ministry, opportunities to be hurt or to hurt others abound. There have been many times in life when what people have said or done has bruised me. Then my whole psyche feels raw, tender and inflamed, needing a spiritual ice pack! It's at times like this that it's good to go to the Deep Place where nobody goes. You will find Him waiting by the refrigerator!

I remember years ago after emigrating, we were trying to adjust to a new country, ministry and language! One difficult situation after another arose. One day I was reading the Golden Book in the Deep Place where nobody goes, before I went out into the shallow places where everyone lives to face some difficult dilemmas. I read Isaiah 42:3.

"You were bruised, but You were never broken," I said to the Lord.

"My Father promised me I should not flag nor break till the work was done," He answered.

"You ploughed Your way through beatings and whippings all the way to Golgotha."

"Bruised but never broken," He said quietly. "What my Father did for Me His Servant, I will do for you 'My' servant."

"I was hoping you would promise me I would never be bruised or broken!"

Then I opened the Golden Book (I always leave one on the Front Door Steps in the Deep Place) and read Isaiah 42 one more time.

"I feel really battered and bruised, Lord," I said when I had finished. "Nothing like You were of course, but it hurts just the same. People in Your church family do awful things to each other. How can this be? It's hard enough fighting the devil and trying to be a light in a dark place, without people in the family of God sidelining you."

I didn't need to say anything else. Like a little child who had just fallen off her bicycle, I held out my life and showed Him all the places I was hurting, and He touched me there. He read my heart prayer.

68

> Touch my stem, Lord,
> Low I bend with bruising;
> Gently now, for I'm your damaged reed.
> Break me not, my Promiser of power,
> Raise not your voice, but rather meet my need.
>
> Speak tenderly, that therapy of caring
> May cool the angry swellings swiftly down,
> Relieve the heat of hurts so deep and crushing
> I in the sea of them am like to drown.
>
> So mend and mould me into stern believing
> That shaped and sharpened, healed and held – a pen I'll be –
> I'll know to write Your words of healed relieving
> Within the hearts and minds of broken men.

So He took my bruisings and mended them. He can, you know. My spirit sat up from its bed of pain and went out boldly into my difficult day. As I went I found myself making up a little song for those I met along the way, and encouraged them to sing it with me. This is how it went.

> Bruised but never broken,
> Down but not destroyed,
> Battered by life's problems,
> Sick or unemployed:
> Struggling with a marriage –
> Rejected we might be –
> Bruised but never broken,
> His promise is for me.

During the difficult day I noticed something else. As I tried to sing this song of help and healing and be a light in a dark place, someone kept trying to snuff out my light! I hastily penned a 'He-mail' to my Heavenly home computer that stands on the steps in the Deep Place where nobody goes: and asked that He would breathe on my dim wick as only He can, that I might shine on. It said:

> Dim my wick is burning,
> Darkness all around:
> Few can see my life-light,
> Faith with doubt is drowned.
> May nail-pierced hands surround me,
> The breath of God breathe low –

My little light flare upwards
And set my life aglow!

He had hardly time to read my message when I felt it. The gentle
breath of God; it was like nothing else! Oh what a day that was
– my heart sang on:

He heals the broken-hearted,
He sets the prisoner free,
Those desperate for forgiveness,
For hope and empathy.
He touches, strengthens, comforts,
And turns their lives about,
Bruised but never broken,
Dim but never out!

Are you bruised? Is your light flickering? Why not borrow my
words?

Breathe on me, breath of God. Mend my bruises, heal my hurts that I do not flag nor fail until my work is done. Breathe on my soul and fan the flames of faith that flicker low. Use me to do your work of healing, till it is needed no more. Thank you that those difficult days make such ministry possible.

Amen

A BOY WAS HE

"THE BOY JESUS STAYED BEHIND IN JERUSALEM…
EVERYONE WHO HEARD HIM WAS AMAZED AT HIS
UNDERSTANDING AND HIS ANSWERS."
Luke 2:43, 47

JESUS NOT ONLY BECAME a baby. He became a boy!

A boy was He
Yet very God of very God,
A child
Yet wiser than His years,
A boy was He
Yet very God of very God
The Lord's own Lamb appears.

A boy was He
Yet very God of very God,
A carpenter's apprentice skilled.

A boy was He
Yet very God of very God
The Lamb, His will fulfills.

Divinity, breathing in air
With a boy's lungs,
Eternity, eating a meal
With a boy's joy.
The Trinity, coming to stay
In a boy's house,
In a boy's pain,
In a boy's world.

A boy was He
Yet very God of very God,
A Son, loved deeply by His own –
A boy was He
Yet very God of very God
The Lamb, so far from home.

Eminence contained,
Immanence experienced,
Holiness explained in a boy!
Truth read clearly,
Love loved dearly,
God known nearly
In a boy!

A boy was He
Yet very God of very God
A child, yet wiser than His years,
A boy was He
Yet very God of very God
The Lord's own Lamb appears.

Christmas

THE ROYAL BIRTHDAY

"BEHOLD, A VIRGIN SHALL BE WITH CHILD AND BRING FORTH
A SON, AND THEY SHALL CALL HIS NAME EMMANUEL,
WHICH BEING INTERPRETED IS, GOD WITH US."
Matthew 1:23 (Authorised Version)

WE WERE CELEBRATING a Royal birthday – His!

It was Christmas Day morning. I went to the Deep Place where nobody goes and looked around. I wondered if He was late because the shining ones, the angels, were giving Him His presents.

While I waited there thinking about that, I began to greatly wonder about the incarnation, and the indescribable gift of a Son born for us on Christmas morning.

Divinity, clothed with humanity – Jesus!

I worshipped that day with words that came easily:

Royal birth!
God in embryo, growing to birth size,
    a baby boy became.
Wrapped in swaddling bands of grace
    a light was lit in a bale of hay,
        setting the world on fire!

They called Him the carpenter's child.
They say He was brought up on
Joseph's knees, playing with a piece of wood.

He went around healing people – mending the world;
Being kind to sinners;
Christ His name…

God in Galilean robes,
dressed for battle – met the devil – paid the price;
WON THE WAR!

Royal birth,
Royal life,
Royal death,
Royal resurrection!

The Front Door opened and though I couldn't see Him (the light was blinding), I knew He was there.

I caught a glimpse of a gigantic Christmas tree, higher than the heavens – in the shape of a cross. There was a star at the top and eastern kings in white robes were pointing to it. The angels were singing carols and I caught some "human words" that sounded familiar. I remembered then that they had been penned on earth; something about…

"Our God contracted in a span
Incomprehensibly made man."

"Glory to God," sang the shining ones – millions of them. Jesus said that that was His best Christmas present! He loves to honour His Father.

I joined in with my whole heart – Christmas had begun!

WINTERMAS

PUT THE BOOK DOWN. It was a wonderful book written by an Englishman, who had had profound things to do with my conversion years ago. It told of winter without Christmas, and how the spring came in the heart of humankind when a lion roared because a baby cried. I read the book most often at Christmas-time when humankind were trying their silly best to celebrate Winter-mas without any spiritual reference to "the Reason for the season". I went to the Deep Place where nobody goes to apologize for the human race.

"It's not your fault," He said comfortingly.

We talked about the week's work. Right up to Christmas Eve night, one after another had found their way to my life to talk about the winter in their souls. It had been pretty depressing.

" Winter came," said one, "stripping my life, icing my soul, drenching my dreams with dark depression."

"What happened?" I asked.

"My husband left me, for a younger model – unmarred by

mothering and managing, worrying and working, and mildewed by middle age!"

Then there was the elderly man who had been faithful to his firm all his life and was due for retirement. He said, "I just lost my job. They are making way for the next generation – don't have to pay them as much! Now I'm redundant and have lost my benefits, and my wife is sick. What about our retirement? I'm a victim of the economy so they say. I suppose they're right. But how will I pay the rent?"

I thought about the stream of people visiting my life – winds howling around the hollow hallway of their souls, their health tenuous, and their relationships frozen solid as ice. And I couldn't help remembering the sad words of the mother of a teenager. "My child doesn't like me very much – well, not at the moment and, if I'm honest, I don't very much like my child! Don't ask me what she's into – I don't want to know. I had such high hopes for her."

Then a sister called me in tears of concern for her brother. The one who came out of the closet – right into their living room, spoiling the Christmas party, shocking the family. "He didn't need to invite his partner!" she sobbed. "It was 'right in our face'!" No, he didn't need to invite him, but then it happens.

Winter came – stripping their lives, freezing their feelings, numbing their minds.

As the wonderful book I was reading said, they were all experiencing a "winter without Christmas"!

So we sat and thought about it all – Him and me. At least, I supposed He was thinking about it, but then He could have been planning the sunshine, counting His angels, or just being God!

"Jill?" I jumped.

"Yes, Lord?"

"Do you remember when the robin's song blessed the bitter wind in your soul and a baby's cry lit up your life, warming your spirit till it stopped shivering and smiled again?"

"Oh Jesus, *yes*! You came into my winter."

"Show them how I can come into theirs."

"I tried."

"I know you did. Keep trying. Call them back – follow up. Once is not enough. I'm the only answer."

"I know." I knew He was right. They had to hear the Lion roar.

Tell them I would wrap them in Divinity's down, Salvation's swaddling bands – insulating them against all the below-zero experiences of life."

"I'll tell them that."

He left then and I picked up the wonderful book and finished it. And I sat very still on the steps of my soul, thanking God for men like C.S. Lewis whose writings walked into my life and caused me to hear the Lion of the tribe of Judah roar, experience the ice melt, and know that springtime had come!

LION OF JUDAH

Lion of Judah, great I AM,
Yet Son of God and gentle lamb;
The One who made all human life,
Yet babe in womb of Joseph's wife.
Majestic One who naked came
To dress Himself in human shame.
Naked twice, in crib, on cross,
Lord of all who suffered loss.
Lion of Judah, great I AM,
Yet Son of God and gentle lamb.

Lion of Judah, great I AM,
Yet Son of God and gentle lamb;
Powerful voice of God most high,
Yet limited to baby's cry.
Mighty Father from above,
Yet needing now a mother's love.

Helper, hope of Israel,
Helpless now, Immanuel.
Lion of Judah, great I AM,
Yet Son of God and gentle lamb.

Lion of Judah, great I AM,
Yet Son of God and gentle lamb;
Majesty displayed in space
Lets me look into His face.
Meekness brings you near today
A Christmas babe in trough of hay.
A mighty God, a tiny child,
Omnipotence so meek and mild.
Lion of Judah, great I AM,
Yet Son of God and gentle lamb.

Lion of Judah, great I AM,
Yet Son of God and gentle lamb
Came to Joseph, shepherd, king,
To those who needed songs to sing;
So hurting women, broken men,
Could find new life, be born again;
Because of Him, the gentle lamb,
Lion of Judah, great I AM!

JESUS, MY SONBEAM

"THE SON IS THE RADIANCE OF GOD'S GLORY AND THE EXACT
REPRESENTATION OF HIS BEING."
Hebrews 1:3

I WAS SITTING IN THE WARM SUNSHINE, thinking about Jesus. I thought about the sun and the way the outshining, or radiance, of it looked like arms of sun-ness coming from the big ball in the sky.

I remembered drawing the sun as a child, and how I would draw it with lines coming out from the big ball of fire. They were the sunbeams. As I grew I learned the sunbeams are of the same essence as the sun itself. They are made of the same stuff!

Then I read in Hebrews about Jesus being of the same essence as God Himself. God is like the sun, Christ is the sunbeam – the radiance of God. He is as much God as God, just as the sunbeam is as much sun as the sun. "Jesus, my Sonbeam," I murmured.

It started with a sunbeam
Bound for a crossbeam
A Sunbeam from the Glory
Shining on the earth.
Beloved of the Father,
Begotten not created
Infinitely precious
Borrowing my birth.

Born a little boy beam
Bound for a crossbeam
Favourite of the Father
Takes a servant's place.
Stripping off his royalty
Robed in humanity
Smile of His Father
With tears on His face.

Birthed in obscurity
Living in poverty
King as a commoner
Revealing God to men.
Carrying my cross for me

All the way to Calvary
Sonbeam a-dying –
Then shining again!

Shine in my darkest days
Teach me to live in praise
Deal with my doubting
And use all my pain.
Mirrored in my mendedness,
Helping all my helplessness
Sonbeam of my Father
Light up my life again!

MEET HIM AT THE MANGER

A manger holds the secret for a world of fear and doubt,
A baby boy lies in the hay, now what's that all about?
Well, the Christian says that God in Christ came down to make
a way
So we could have our sins forgiven and go to heaven one day.

How could God lie unvisited while Beth'lem passed on by,
And people that first Christmas day ignored a baby's cry?
Well, they were busy partying and seeing family
So what's the difference in our world of cruel neglect to be?

The shepherds did their best to tell the world and do their part
They met Him at the manger, and they let Him have their
heart.
And kings that came to worship, and risk King Herod's fury
Returned to tell their land of Him and His salvation story.

Right: Bethlehem, Jesus' birth place

So why not bring your mind to bear on God's great gift of
    grace,
And as you watch sweet Mary wipe the tears from His face,
Resolve to seek with all your soul the Christ who gave it all:
The gift of Incarnation, within that cattle stall!

Lord, may we meet You at the manger of our hearts.

Amen

THE OVERSHADOWING

" 'How will this be,' Mary asked the Angel, 'since I am a virgin?' The Angel answered, 'The Holy Spirit will come upon you, and the power of the Most High will overshadow you.' "

Luke 1:34–35 (Authorised Version)

Have you ever felt overwhelmed? That life is just too much? Too heavy the demands, too painful the problems, too daunting the task? Then hurry to the Deep Place where nobody goes.

I remember such a day. I was overwhelmed. It wasn't one thing but many. Suddenly, one morning, I didn't want to get out of bed. So I stayed there for a bit and went and sat down in the Deep Place, on the steps of my soul. You can, you know, even when you're in bed!

"I'm overwhelmed," I announced loud and clear, expecting Him to come running. He didn't. I hung around for half an hour or so and became gradually aware of a sweet darkening of the windows of my soul. It was as if someone had drawn the curtains to help a sick child rest better. I lay still.

"I'm overwhelmed," I said, quietly this time. No need to

shout; did not He whom my soul loves say, "My ear is not heavy that it cannot hear"?

The sweet safe shadow around me deepened. Then His voice said clearly, "When you're overwhelmed, remember that you are overshadowed!"

Oh! So that was it. The Overshadowing! I was "under His wings".

I remembered Mary, and reaching for my Bible read a little of her Christmas story and how the beautiful angel came and told her he had come to interrupt all her really personal plans for her life with Joseph. When told she would be the mother of Messiah, she had asked a very practical question. "How?"

"That was a brave question," I said out loud.

"Yes," He replied, close at hand. "She was very brave. She didn't ask 'Why me?' she asked, 'How me?' She was overwhelmed with the 'How shall this be, seeing I know not a man?'"

"I can only understand such a small fraction of what she felt," I said. "But I can relate to her sense of inadequacy. That's my problem right now. How can I do so much, care so much, work so much, love so much, travel so much, forgive so much, give so much? It's all so much 'much'! I'm overwhelmed!"

"I told you – " He began.

"Yes, yes," I interrupted Him. "I know. When I'm overwhelmed, I've to remember I'm overshadowed. But – but, Lord Jesus – just what do you mean?" Then the wonderful shadow seemed to wrap itself around me and hold me close into

God, as if it were a warm, comforting heavenly blanket.

"The Holy Spirit," He said, knowing I needed no more talk, just touch.

"The Comforter."

"Yes, the Comforter. That's what Gabriel told my mother, when she was overwhelmed. 'The Holy Spirit will overshadow you,' and ever after when she was overwhelmed she remembered she was overshadowed." Wrapped warmly in that same promise and reality, I got up and went out into my day.

The challenges hadn't changed, but I clothed myself in "a garment of Praise" that covered over my "Spirit of heaviness". It would be all right. I vowed to keep the conversation in mind. When I was overwhelmed, I would believe that I was overshadowed.

Oh Lord of all Comfort, comfort me.

Oh God of all might, strengthen me.

Oh Lord of all Joy, I praise your Holy

name. Behold your servant – be it

unto me according to your word!

Amen

ROSES

WHEN YOU CAN'T GET HOME FOR CHRISTMAS

"YOU KNOW THE GRACE OF OUR LORD JESUS CHRIST, THAT
THOUGH HE WAS RICH, YET FOR YOUR SAKES HE BECAME POOR,
THAT YOU THROUGH HIS POVERTY MIGHT BECOME RICH."
2 Corinthians 8:9

IT'S HARD WHEN YOU CAN'T get home to be with family for Christmas, Thanksgiving, or a special birthday.

Jesus' birthday was coming up. Christmas was just around the corner. "What should I give Him" I wondered? I thought about flowers and suddenly that triggered a vivid memory of a meeting in Singapore, where a veteran missionary had shared an experience on the mission field. It was to do with trying to get home, not for Christmas but for his mother's 90th birthday. Because of a crisis, and the primitive circumstances in which he worked (he had a leadership role in the mission) it was impossible to get away. It broke his heart.

"That must have hurt," I pondered as I listened to him. How

difficult both for him and his mother. It hurts so badly when those we love can't get home for the holidays. Well, I thought, at least Jesus will be home for Christmas this year! He wasn't always able to make it. For 33 years it was impossible. He had a leadership role in the mission!

The missionary told us how he had the brilliant idea of sending his mother ten roses each hour of her birthday till she had received all 90. He tied a "Thank you" note to each rose, and sent her a card with the first batch of ten. It said: "How do I love you, let me count the ways." Then he thought of 90 ways he loved his mother and attached a different thank you to every rose!

"I'll do that," I decided. So I bought a big bunch of roses, went to the Deep Place where nobody goes and sat down on the steps. If I stayed still enough I could hear angels singing carols – practising. Pretty.

"Hullo."

I jumped. "Oh! Hullo, I thought I'd get ahead of the rush."

He looked at the roses in my hands and I resisted the urge to give Him the whole bunch at once and return to the mall to continue my shopping. (I did have a busy day ahead of me – after all, Christmas was coming.)

I began taking the roses one by one and, carefully attaching a message to each, I said loudly, so He could hear me: " How do I love Thee, let me count the ways", and then I began to count them. I wanted above all to thank Him for being willing "not" to get home for Christmas for 33 years.

He sat there – relaxed (he must have done all His shopping already) and He looked serious and focused. (I love that.) He accepted each offering into His hands – I tried not to look at the scars. (I hate that.)

"I love you for sitting on the steps with me in the Deep Place where nobody goes," I began, handing Him a flower. "And I love it that you always follow me up the steps and remind me you are there in the shallow places where everyone lives – even though I forget you're there in all the commotion.

"And I love you for coming to earth and walking straight into my heart – and making this woman yours for ever. And oh how I love you for becoming poor so I could become rich beyond measure. Yes, yes, Lord, that I through your poverty could become rich! I love you, I love you, I love you!"

Rose by rose I thanked him, telling Him all the ways I loved Him, and then the bunch of flowers was in His hands and mine were empty. I cried – happy grateful tears, and watched in amazement as each tear became a rose petal strewn at His feet.

He bent down, holding my roses carefully, gathering my flowers of love and thankfulness into His scarred hands, saying quietly, "Not one of these shall fall to the ground." Then He looked at me with eyes so full of love I thought I would die. Then He was gone.

I heard the church bells ringing then, and knew I had to return to the shallow places where everyone lives. I did so reluctantly, knowing the party was about to begin. Christmas was coming!

How do I love Thee? Let me
count the ways: "One..."

THE DEEP PLACE WHERE NOBODY GOES

ROSES IN DECEMBER

Roses in December,
Lord, you are to me
Bringing life and fragrance
Sweet vitality.
Blooming when I'm jaded,
Lacking joy and power,
Jesus, Rose of Sharon,
God's most precious flower.

Roses in December,
Fragrance of the One
Whose petals bore the dew of death
When my salvation won.
Crushed by death's endeavour
And the punishment you bore,
Jesus, Rose of Sharon,
Thee I do adore!

Roses in December,
In our darkest hours,
Soul and body freeing
From death's gruesome powers.
When our days are dreary;
And when the winter starts,
Jesus, Rose of Sharon,
Bloom within our hearts!

ONLY GOD CAN PAINT A ROSE

"[HE IS:] 'THE ROSE OF SHARON'"

Song of Songs 2:1

∽ ⁓

HER NAME WAS CARMEN. My sweet friend.

She lay still, shadows deepening outside the Front Door, the setting sun casting a long shadow on the steps. Death drew the drapes.

She was a neighbourly neighbour, greeting our family, newly arrived from England, with a hot delicious meal and a smile that could charm a duck off water! It didn't take long till she was loving our kids and making them hers – Aunty Carmen.

She walked into my life and helped me settle into this strange country far from my England: "Thank you, Lord, for Carmen!"

Made in His image – an artist, and a good one – she came to faith. What a day!

At once she, and others, noticed a difference in her art. Once captured by her Jesus, her brush fairly flew over the canvas, discovering myriad ways to reflect His beauty. Mostly it was roses she loved. And why not, I ask you? I'm English, I understand her wonder! After all, only God can paint a rose!

She was only a day or so short of walking through the Front Door. As the shadows lengthened we were sure we could see incredible light, like nothing on earth, through the crack!

"Make me a poem for the funeral, Jill," she asked me with the little breath she had left.

"Oh Carmen, I… I don't think… "

"Please."

"Of course!"

I left her then, turning at the door to say goodnight, but her eyes were closed. She was smiling. I could tell she had her hand on the latch.

The phone call came very soon. I ran to the Deep Place where nobody goes and found Him holding some rose stems with the most gorgeous blooms. The flowers were incredibly beautiful, but I noticed he had pricked His finger: the blood was deep and red.

"No rose without thorns, Jill – this side of heaven."

"No Lord, so it seems."

"She asked me… " I began.

"… To write a poem for the funeral," He finished.

" I don't know how… "

"I'll help," He said softly.

It was much, much later when I finished. I sat still thinking of Carmen's brave descent through the pain and parting, and I cried. Thorns hurt.

When I arrived at the funeral home I stepped inside and

gasped. The family had transported her beautiful art and displayed it all around the room. By her coffin stood an easel and 'The rose of roses'. It was her prize piece of art. "He is my Rose of Sharon," she had told me once. I had not known I would be standing by that painting by her coffin when He had helped me put pen to paper in the early morning hours, but He had. Somehow, with His help, I got through the poem when my turn came. What a privilege.

Greatest God and Heavenly Artist,
See our sense of loss and grief,
Speak a word of heavenly comfort,
Bring a breath of sweet relief.
On the canvas of our memories
Framed in thoughts of years past
Dip your brush in "Carmen colours" –
Paint a portrait that will last.

Picture of a cherished mother ,
Precious daughter, wife and friend,
Aunt and mentor, Jesus lover,
He her Master, Saviour, Friend!
Tears are over, grief forgotten,
Joy now swells and fills her soul,
Loving God defuses anguish,
Body, soul and mind makes whole.

Carmen, new dimension living,
Purposeful existence knows,
Seeing God prepare His palette,
Watching Jesus paint a rose.
Brushing sunsets with light colours,
Misting meadows with His breath,
Praising Him in exultation,
Carmen laughs with God at death!

Precious dear one, missed already
As your dear ones mourn your loss,
May your death be our reminder
We can join you through your cross!
Door to life, Christ's rich atonement,
Gift of love His tomb displays,
Cost God's Son His death to open
Heaven's joys to one who prays.

On the canvas of our memories
Framed Oh God in years to be,
Dip your brush in "Carmen colours"
Paint a picture just for me.
Carmen, vibrant life enjoying,
Perfect health and wholeness knows,
Watches God prepare His colours
Helps her Jesus paint a rose!

ELDERLY LADIES AND GENTLEMEN

"JOSEPH BROUGHT HIS FATHER JACOB IN AND PRESENTED HIM
BEFORE PHARAOH... PHARAOH ASKED HIM,
"HOW OLD ARE YOU?"
AND JACOB SAID TO PHARAOH, "THE YEARS OF MY PILGRIMAGE
ARE A HUNDRED AND THIRTY. MY YEARS HAVE BEEN FEW AND
DIFFICULT, AND THEY DO NOT EQUAL THE YEARS OF THE
PILGRIMAGE OF MY FATHERS."

Genesis 47:7–9

105

JOSEPH WAS INTRODUCING HIS ancient father to the King of Egypt. Pharaoh said to Jacob, "How old are you?" He was amazed at the 130-odd years Jacob was carrying. Living that long was a wonder to the Egyptians at that time, as their writings attest.

Jacob replied that he was a mere babe compared to his forebears who had lived hundreds of years longer than he had. Jacob apparently never thought of himself as an elderly gentleman!

Shortly after reading about Jacob, I had cause to think about the question myself. I was running out of our church building into the bitter Wisconsin winter, trying not to let the Lord see my thoughts about His weather! I had not taken time to put on my winter boots. Suddenly, I skidded on a patch of black ice and before I could stop myself, my feet slipped from under me and my legs went right over my head!

Because my hands were full I didn't put them out to save myself, so I landed right on the top of my head and knocked myself out! Stuart, who was with me at the time, looked at me lying there peacefully, and was about to leap into husbandly action when a young man nearby (the only other person in the icy parking lot) whipped out his mobile phone and called for an ambulance.

I came to hearing him say, "An elderly lady has just fallen in the car park!" My first and immediate thought was: Isn't that amazing! Someone else has fallen in the car park at exactly the same time as me! It never occurred to me for a minute to recognize myself in his description but then, as I said to the Lord as they whipped me around the hospital X-raying everything, "How could he have been talking about me? I am *not* an elderly lady!"

As I lay still after all the tests and listened to my husband and the emergency doctor discussing me as if I wasn't there, I again wondered greatly. Could they be talking about me? How could this be?

"Watch for unusual signs," the doctor advised my husband.

"Like what?" asked Stuart.

"Forgetfulness, not finishing sentences… "

"Or finishing mine for me?" Stuart interjected.

"Confusion – forgetting where her car is parked… "

As the man continued to describe my life before the blow on the head, my husband enquired whether there was any chance – if this behaviour was normal – that a blow on the head could reverse it?

The doctor looked a little startled but only for a second. He quickly replied that if Stuart saw such a thing he was to call him immediately and he would write it up for the medical books. Then we went home.

As I nursed the huge egg on my head for the next few days, I had reason to think about this "elderly lady" thing. You know I *am* an elderly lady – pushing 70 – and it is still a wonder to me that, as my husband loves to say so often on his "elderly gentleman" birthdays, "How can someone as young as me be as old as this?"

The answer to all of these questions is, of course, that God has promised that "as the outer man perishes the inner man is renewed day by day". It's true. Yes, it's true!

So I went to the Deep Place where no one goes (I have to watch myself on the steps of my soul these days, just as I do in the icy parking lot!) to thank Him for the gift of eternal life that never ages!

I spent time studying His word that day and after quite a while reading in all sorts of places, realized He whom my soul loves had left me a message within its pages:

The soul doesn't age, gifts don't age, and a heart for Me is

renewed moment by moment and day by day. I will energize

you, strengthen your bones, and freshen your soul!

Love,

God

I scribbled a reply and left it for him in the Deep Place. Then I went back to the shallow place where everyone lives and went for a lovely walk with my "elderly gentleman"!

Thank you, dear Heavenly Companion and sweet friend, that you have counted out my days and the years of my pilgrimage. I will spend all my days and all my hours for you.

Love,

Jill

JESUS LOVERS AND GLORY GIVERS

"Since my youth, O God, you have taught me, and to this day I declare your marvellous deeds. Even when I am old and grey, do not forsake me, O God, till I declare your power to the next generation."

Psalm 71:17–18

Do you ever feel your age? Years ago, in Japan in the middle of an exhausting itinerary, I woke one morning really cross. It wasn't fair. If God wanted me to do all this hard travel and work why didn't He ask me when I was 23, not 63? I dragged myself out of bed and made a cup of tea (which English ladies who are 63 always do first thing in the morning).

Somewhat reluctantly I went to the Deep Place where nobody goes and sat on the steps of my soul, clutching my cup of tea. (I noticed that the older I got the harder it was getting to "sit" on the steps of my soul!)

"Bad morning, God," I said, " I've woken up grumpy!"

"Why is that?"

"I'm feeling my age – I'm 63 you know."

"I know! What's the matter with your age? How old would you like to be?"

"50."

"Why do you want to be 50?"

"It's better than 63, I told him. "63 is so-o-o-o old!"

"It's not too old."

"Too old for what?"

"Too old to love Me, too old to serve Me. Too old to delight in Me!'

"But I don't want to be 63. I feel like an *Old*-age pensioner, a *Senior* citizen, a – *Grand*mother – a *Veteran* veteran – "

"Well, at 63 you are a veteran! And that's that. What's more, at the moment you are a 63-year-old veteran grump!"

"I don't want to be a grump!"

"Then stop it!"

"How?"

"Choose."

"Choose what? Ooo – can I choose not to be 63?"

"No! But you can choose what 'sort' of a 63-year-old you can be! A 63-year-old veteran grump, or a 63-year-old Jesus Lover and Glory Giver! Think a while. Think of the veteran Jesus Lovers you know. You've been among many on this trip. Some are even older than you!"

"Some as in 'very few'? "

"Don't you want to be like them?"

"Yes."

"Then start."

"How?"

"What do you like about them?"

"Mmm." I hesitated.

Then He whom my soul loves gave me a pen and paper and I saw He had written down the edge of the paper. Looking closer I saw the letters of an acrostic: V.E.T.E.R.A.N.

I knew He expected me to fill it in with the character elements of Jesus Lovers and Glory Givers who were old like me. So I shut my eyes and thought about all the missionaries and church leaders I had met on the trip. Then I wrote:

Very determined. They had a sort of set to their spiritual chin that said, "I *will* finish the work You gave me to do."

Excited about Jesus.

Tired! Too much to do and not enough hands to the pump. Yet you can see they are only tired "*in*" the work of the Lord, not "*of*" it – there's a difference.

Enthusiastic about the people they serve – even the weird ones! *And* **E**nergetic! Really! Even though their bodies are weary. Something about the dynamic energy of the Holy Spirit, they say.

Rich beyond measure. You can see it in their eyes! And they are so ridiculously happy. Not just "happy-clappy" but heart happy – all the time. But then Joy is Jesus – and the "Joy of the Lord is their strength."

Appreciating the simple things in life – birdsong, a child's laughter; sunrise and sunset; clean air and water; their daily bread. And they…

Never stop nurturing their relationship with God – determining to know Him better today than yesterday.

He was back. I made room for Him on the steps.
    "So what's it to be, Jill?"

"Choose time?"

"Choose time!"

"OK, let's start again. Good morning, God. It's me, Jill. I'm your 63-year-old veteran (smile, a bit forced, but it was a start) Jesus Lover and Glory Giver. Let's go."

And we did!

Lord, forgive my moans and groans. Thank you for the measure of health I have, and help me to use it to encourage the weak, strengthen the doubters, challenge the wayward, and keep helping the helpless. Give me love for You and love for them! Help me, however many birthdays I have left, to finish the work you gave me to do! Even when I'm old and grey, help me to declare your power to the next generation.

Amen

TODAY

"THEREFORE DO NOT WORRY ABOUT TOMORROW,
FOR TOMORROW WILL WORRY ABOUT ITSELF. EACH DAY
HAS ENOUGH TROUBLE OF ITS OWN."
Matthew 6:34

❧

MY BACK WAS PLAYING UP. The pain was pretty grim. I had lots of physical work to do and I didn't know how I was going to manage. But the problem wasn't really today: it was tomorrow!

Tomorrow I had to get myself to the airport and travel. I had to lift my suitcase into the car, sit a long time in the aeroplane and go in a bumpy taxi to the church where I was speaking. There I would need to stand all day to teach, sit on church chairs (the worst!) and then travel back at the end of the day.

"'Then' is tomorrow. 'Now' is today and 'Now' is all you have." I heard Him say. "Today, the pain is not so bad, be grateful. In faith, determine that today shall be a good day."

So I spent a little time "determining". Then I made a list.

> Today –
>   I will greet friends,

Work on work,
Cook a little,
Laugh a lot,
Watch my favourite team on TV.

I will plan for the next ten hours
only
but carefully –
Trying to pack the precious given
moments full
of good things to do.
Today is going to be quite
achievable.

Then I dared to peep around the corner of
tomorrow for just a moment of time.

Tomorrow may not be quite so
achievable –
But, hallelujah, tomorrow is not
today.
The "then'" is not the "now"
And I don't need to live it yet!

I found a really nice greeting card that I could pin
to God's Front Door in the Deep Place where
nobody goes. I wrote:

Dear Lord,

May I but know, with utmost certainty, that I will find you waiting around the corner of tomorrow with my future in your hands. I know You will not hold it lightly – for You have whispered to my heart that I am infinitely precious to You. Yes, in all my tomorrows You will help me to manage the pain, and I am glad! See you there, Jill

GOLD FAITH

"[JESUS] TOOK A LITTLE CHILD… [AND] TAKING HIM IN HIS
ARMS, HE SAID TO THEM, 'WHOEVER WELCOMES ONE OF THESE
LITTLE CHILDREN IN MY NAME WELCOMES ME;
AND WHOEVER WELCOMES ME DOES NOT WELCOME ME
BUT THE ONE WHO SENT ME."
Mark 9:36–37

∾

IT WAS TIME TO GO TO the dedication service for one of our grandsons. I ran to the Deep Place where nobody goes. Sitting still I thought about the miracle of "Life begetting life" – a gift of grace and mercy beyond imagining. And now another little eternal person had been given to us:

"Lord, I want to thank you for the safe birth and the perfect child you graced us with. So many prayers answered. We welcome him."

"My pleasure."

"They asked me to write the prayer of dedication; would you help me with the words?"

Later, I took the piece of paper, wet with tears of gratitude, and read the words out among the ones we love best upon this earth:

Father dear,
Whose very nature is to care
see us here,
Your own forever family,
Suspended in time and space,
turning our thoughts towards
Thee.

Father Dear,
Whose very nature is to love,
So fan the flames of all our
family relationships,
that they may be a warm place
where children love to play.
Where people live to give each other
room to breathe and space to grow.

Father Dear,
Whose very nature is to give,
teach us what that means.
That Jesus, Saviour of our lives
may lend His power of giving
to our selfish hearts.

Father Dear,
Whose very nature is to overcome,
we face the forces

marching on our homes
with cruel intent to harm us.
We peep behind the drapes of dread
drawn tight across our future dreams
and shudder at the menace of men's ways.

We know not what to do,
Fight for us,
You are our mighty conqueror.

Protect our little ones,
And lend us weaponry to reinforce
our souls with the muscles
of Your might
faith
hope
and love.

And, Oh dear Teacher,
So show us how to model Christ in all
His sweet simplicity and strength –
that seeing Him in us our children shall inherit
gold faith,
Trust tried in the crucible of life,
our gift to them –
a godly heritage!
Amen

Father Dear, teach
us that the greatest
gift we can give to
our children is to be
made in the likeness
of Christ ourselves.

Amen

NOT THE WAY THINGS OUGHT TO BE

"IN KEEPING WITH HIS PROMISE WE ARE LOOKING FORWARD
TO A NEW HEAVEN AND A NEW EARTH, THE HOME
OF RIGHTEOUSNESS."

2 Peter 3:13

What has blotted out the blue of the sky? Whose face comes to mind? What happened to make things "Not the way they ought to be" in your life? When did the tsunami or the hurricane hit? Are there sustained winds? Is it a category five? What extraordinary crisis is yours? I know how you feel!

"Lord," I whispered, "it's not the way things ought to be!"

I had come to the Deep Place troubled beyond measure. "I had so many hopes and dreams," I told Him, "Now they will never be realized."

"So did I."

"You had dreams never realized?" I asked in surprise.

"Of course. Did you imagine this sorry world is all I dreamed for you? It's not the way things ought to be!"

He handed me a pencil and paper. "Write your pain away," He suggested. I knew that worked – it was a secret way for me to use the therapy of writing to cool my overheated heart. As I wrote, praise rose unbidden – a welcome guest!

It's not the way things ought to be
And yet the way things are,
I look above and see a void
And not one single star.
Then in the day the blue is grey,
The winds of change are stilled,
My heart it seems
Must die to dreams
I'll never see fulfilled.

It's not the way things ought to be
And yet the way things are,
Then God walks in,
Forgives the sin
And lights my evening star.
He tames my rebel doubts with love,
Rebukes my frantic fears,
Then asks me why
I sigh and cry
And counts my many tears.

One day the things that "ought to be"
Will be the way He's planned,
So I should live
And freely give
My hopes into His hand.
I'll live in light of ever-ness
With eyes upon the Throne,
He'll give me grace
To run the race
Till I am safely home.

Lord Jesus, Lighten my load, light up my life,
Walk around my grief and send it packing –

Help me to sing my pain away.
Strengthen my faith so I can live in the good of things
to come before they're here. That's the faith you ask for –
may I not be wanting in giving it to You. Amen

DOING YESTERDAY

⟨⟩

*S*OME SAY YOU CAN'T RELIVE YESTERDAY, but I beg to differ! You can live it in your mind as vividly as when it was indeed yesterday itself! I know – I do it all the time.

I woke up one morning and before I could start "doing today" began "doing yesterday" with a vengeance. Do you "do yesterday" as well as I do? Whereas fear is the driving dynamic of "doing tomorrow"; guilt and shame are often the driving force of "doing yesterday".

I didn't go to talk about it in the Deep Place this time as I find that He doesn't like to let me talk much about the past. It's usually "today" and sometimes "tomorrow" we focus on. Of course, it's all the same to Him as not only is He "the same yesterday, today and forever", but He lives in all three dimensions all at the same time! God is so clever!

However, I didn't particularly want to talk to Him about yesterday as I sort of guessed what He'd say, and I didn't want to hear it. So I went for a walk and talked to my soul about it all on our own. As soon as I began whingeing about yesterday – which is what I really wanted to do, have a good old whinge – a soft footfall alerted me to His sweet presence! I'd forgotten the Deep Place is within me!

"Hullo!"

"Er, hullo."

"Who were you talking to?"

"Me!"

"Were you having a good conversation?"

(Reprovingly) "Well, I'd only just begun!"

(Cheerfully) "Good, time I got in on the conversation!"

I was quiet, wondering how to proceed.

"I was just thinking – " I began.

"You were thinking you'd take a trip down memory lane."

"Yes. I was wondering what would have happened if I'd said the right thing, or if I'd never gone there that fateful day, or if I'd had the common sense to… ". And then as the memories flooded back as vividly as if it had all just happened, drowning me, and causing my stomach to go into a knot as I relived the awful situation, I burst out with, "Why didn't you stop me saying it, Lord?"

"You are responsible for what comes out of your mouth, Jill."

"You shut the mouths of the lions, Lord – you could surely have shut mine!"

"You are not a wild animal, Jill. You are a Christian who knows that power is made available to you to say or stay – to speak or forbear."

"But what is said is said – I can't take it back: wish it unsaid, or take the words from the mind of the person I was speaking to."

"True. So stop trying to take back what is said and done. That's futile. Keep your energy for today."

"How?"

"Live in the moment. It's the only thing you have!"

"How?"

"You mind your mind – I'll mind your heart!"

Lord of my yesterdays, forgive me. I'll mind my mind: I'll stop "playing the tape". Please, Lord, don't let the tormenting memories control my mood and actions. Mind my heart. Amen

THE DEEP PLACE WHERE NOBODY GOES

DOING TODAY

"YOU WILL COME TO THE GRAVE IN FULL VIGOUR,
LIKE SHEAVES GATHERED IN SEASON"

Job 5:26

❧

AVE YOU EVER HAD A TIME in your life when you couldn't face what the day would bring? I have – like today. Then I go to the Deep Place where nobody goes. He who has already visited all my tomorrows knows what today will bring forth. He is not beaten down – not bowed over, bent low like a sheaf of grain in a wind storm. Not like me.

"How do I 'do today', Lord? It's too long, too hard – "

"Life won't go on without you?"

"No. But I can't do today! Pain takes my breath. The things that matter most to me are crumbling. Help!"

"I am here. Come – "

"I can't 'do today' "

"I can!"

"I'm not God – that's the problem."

"I Am."

"I believe! But dear Lord, I can't do today – even half a day."

"Do this minute."

Difficult days

"I don't think...."

"Yes you can, you can do the next minute. Try, count the seconds: One, two, three – "

Silence.

"Now the next one. I have counted out your moments and your days for you already. Now you do it."

"But that first minute lasted so long!"

"This time stop counting and read a verse of Scripture: fill the next minute thinking about Me."

Then I read Job 5:26: "You will come to the grave in full vigour, like sheaves gathered in season."

"Lord, I feel beaten down like a sheaf in a wind storm."

"Here comes the sun! You and I will 'do today' together."

Silence.

I put my hand into His, and counting hard, "did

today". "Lord of all my yesterdays and tomorrows: help me to 'do today'," I asked Him. "My sheaf bends in the wind."

"Till I gather you into my barn you must bend in the winds that come: for you must stand in the harvest field until it is your season. It will not blow so hard today. In the respite wait patiently. Rest in Me. One day, 'today' as I intended it, will come to be."

Then I began to climb the steps to the shallow place where everyone lives and found "today" happening. I counted every other step and tried to think of a promise. On the alternate step I said loudly, "I believe!" And when I just couldn't take another step I breathed, "Help thou mine unbelief!"

> *Lord, sometimes I have no more strength to cope: However hard the wind blows, give me the spiritual vigour I need to serve you today. Amen*

DOING TOMORROW

"DO NOT WORRY ABOUT TOMORROW,
FOR TOMORROW WILL WORRY ABOUT ITSELF. EACH DAY
HAS ENOUGH TROUBLE OF ITS OWN."
Matthew 6:34

HAVE YOU EVER BEEN UNABLE to cope today because of what you fear will happen tomorrow? I was sitting on the steps of my soul, "doing tomorrow". I began thinking about all the worst-case scenarios that could happen in a certain situation.

"Doing tomorrow" has different challenges from "Doing today". I should know, I seem to have been "Doing tomorrow" before I have "done today" all of my life! And this robs me of the strength for "doing today". I've noticed that in the Deep Place it is always "today". You can't go there tomorrow. It is the ever-living present.

That's good, because He said, "Each day has enough troubles of its own." He was sitting still on the steps beside me.

"That sounds familiar," I replied. "What happens if – if – "

"I told you to stop thinking about tomorrow."

"But I can't. What if – ?"

"Jill, you have to stop this."

"But the dreaded tomorrow is about to happen Lord. I can't just walk into it without having a contingency plan – or two, or three. What if –?"

"The problem is if you engage in this useless speculation you will find yourself living in the day after tomorrow!" He said, smiling gently.

"What do you mean?"

"You will start by saying, 'What will happen if?' Then you will get into: 'When what happens tomorrow surely happens (of that you have convinced yourself) – what then?' And then your mind will jump to the next day and the next. Then you will be convinced the day after tomorrow will be worse than the day before tomorrow, and the next a disaster, and the next.… "

"It's true!" I cried. "Oh Lord, it's like a momentum takes over and the apprehension grows and grows."

"Most of your fears will never happen."

I jumped on that. "I know, Lord, but though 'most' will not, 'some' of them will, won't they? So what if the fears I most fear are the ones that do? What then?"

"Stop it! You have emptied today of its strength already with all this worry!"

Well, that was true. I was near tears all the time. Earlier that week when the gardener came to ask me what I wanted to do with the flowerbed I just gazed at him uncomprehendingly. He looked at me apprehensively and murmured, "We need to get to the weeds." That jerked me back to today, and I burst into tears!

The poor man looked aghast. I couldn't cope – I didn't know what to tell him to do about the weeds. I had no ideas left as I had been busy living in the scenarios I had convinced myself would follow my dark today!

I stood there weeping quietly as the poor man removed himself to the far corner of the garden, fell to his knees and began ripping out the weeds! What had he done to upset me? he must have been thinking. The offending weeds weren't that bad!

I looked at Him desperately. "Tell me to stop it," I asked Him.

"Stop it," He said. "Do not worry about tomorrow, for tomorrow will worry about itself."

Well, now, I thought: if tomorrow was going to worry about itself, I needn't worry about it as well!

"I will be obedient, Lord," I said contritely. "Help me."

"I will meet you around the corner of your tomorrow with your future in My hands." He said. "We will meet it when it comes, you and I together. That is all you need to know. Now, about today… "

Doing tomorrow is exhausting, Lord. You have to live all the problems out, feel the pain of them in advance, and then worry about all the repercussions! When You say, "stop it!" help me to listen. Forbid me to peer into a scary future expecting the worst. Only You can change my focus. Step by daily step, teach me to "do today"!

Amen

A MORNING WITHOUT CLOUDS

ASKED MYSELF, "Why do my days dawn in dreariness? Why do I worry so?" Do you ever ask yourself these questions? Do you seem to be living under a cloud? After reading, in the Scripture, "When shall I arise and the night be ended?" I went to the Deep Place where nobody goes to talk to Him about it and ask, "Indeed when?" I noticed as soon as I arrived that the sun was shining!

"Lord!" I exclaimed. "Why do I wake up every day and feel like midnight when it's dawn?" I knew this verse spoke of Christ's Second Coming that would one day be like waking to "a morning without clouds", yet I also knew in my heart I should be living in the light of that promise now.

"So why do I live under a cloud, Lord?" I asked. "Is it because I'm English?" He laughed. I didn't, because you don't laugh much when you live under a cloud!

Then he said simply: "The morning comes."

I realized that the Bible says two seemingly contradictory things. It says "the night comes" and "the morning comes" – "A morning without clouds".

"It all depends if you are a child of darkness or a child of light! It's all truth," He said quietly. "When I say: 'The night comes when no man can work,' that means you should cultivate a sense of urgency and keep focused on the task in hand – namely the work I have given you to do before 'The Day' dawns and the shadows flee away."

"Oh." My mind started to race around the concepts. I began to remember all sorts of other "cloud" verses. I noted briefly I couldn't recall any sunshine verses! "There I go again," I said out loud, "that's how I am – living under a cloud, thinking under a cloud, watching the clouds gather – I never leave home without my umbrella!"

"That's because you're English." He said. This time I laughed.

"What about the verse that says, 'He that regards the clouds will not reap?'" He asked.

"Where's that?" I enquired, interested.

"Never mind 'where' it is, think about 'what' it is: a warning!"

"Well that I get."

"You are supposed to be reaping," He reminded me. "It's hard when all you are doing is watching the clouds and fearing the mother of all storms. You're distracted from the job in hand."

I sat still, thinking about it. The Son felt warm on my soul!

"Well, this is where I need to live," I reflected. Sitting here in my mind in the Son-shine all day long, while I get on with business, His business.

I opened the book of reflections I was reading and read: "But let those who love Him be like the sun when it comes out in full strength." I looked up, startled, and found Him there – so bright, so beautiful, my Jesus! No clouds here in the Deep Place – only clouds of glory!

I thought about the day ahead of me. There were plenty of dark clouds gathering "upstairs" in the shallow places where everyone lives. I had four friends in dire straits in hospital and hospice. One family was at the other end of the country gathered round a close friend on the way to his "coronation day". I had said, "Till we meet again" on the phone the night before. The others, nearer at hand, were in pain, in need of the warm rays of the God we all knew as the "Light of the world".

Today I would visit each one. I wished Stuart could come with me, but he was in Cuba. Though what was ahead for my friends was all joy – getting through the Front Door can be an excruciating challenge sometimes. How could I enter those hospital rooms under a cloud? My friends didn't need that!

Sitting in the Deep Place I tried to look at the gathering storm in my mind's eye, but couldn't seem to find the clouds. He reminded me, "This place knows only light."

"Help me then, sweet Lord of my life, to walk in the light and not in the darkness today."

"You are a child of the light," He reminded me. "Reflect me."

As I set about the ministry of the day I got ready to shine. I disciplined myself not to look at the grey sky waiting for me. I wanted with all my heart to "be about my Father's business".

Lord, the sky lowers, but You shine through –
Oh, what a pretty rainbow!

Difficult days

HIND'S FEET

"THE SOVEREIGN LORD IS MY STRENGTH;
HE MAKES MY FEET LIKE THE FEET OF A DEER,
HE ENABLES ME TO GO ON THE HEIGHTS."
Habakkuk 3:19

∽

*E*ARLY IN THE MORNING as day was dawning, I read Habakkuk. I was glad to arrive at the end of the book. It was so sad. It talked of pain and sorrow, tears and war. But there in chapter four, at the end of the prophecy, I found a song of joy crowning the prophet's psalm of sorrow. Seeing it was early, I went to the Deep Place where nobody goes and waited in the mellow mists of morning to talk to Him about it.

"Habakkuk was my friend," He said quietly. I thought I knew why.

"I think Habakkuk pictured you as the 'Hind of the morning'," I commented. "That's a lovely picture of You." We were quiet, thinking of how at Calvary, the lion got the Hind. I thought of how the devil ripped the Hind to shreds, and shuddered.

"But on Easter morning I got the lion," He said suddenly! And then we laughed, and time stood still and all the trees of the fields clapped their hands.

"Oh dear One, more precious to me than any other, help me to be like you – like a hind, sure-footed on hard ground," I pleaded.

I thought of the challenges that awaited me. Today, I could lose a friend, and even make an enemy for life. Today, I must confront wrongdoing, be misunderstood, play peacemaker between warring factions in the church. Some of my close relationships were at an all-time low!

I didn't like this part of the mountain climb, this part of life and ministry.

"Remember, the low places of life are really the high places of spiritual experience," He reminded me.

"Well then, oh Heavenly Hind of the morning, today, when I find myself picking my way among the rocks and crags, trying to keep my feet and not fall, help me keep my balance."

"I will give you hind's feet in high places if you ask me to," He replied quietly. "I will enable you to go on the heights."

And then we were walking together in the shallow places where everybody lives, looking up at the impossible crags on the mountainside, and they looked for all the world like all the dangerous difficulties of the day ahead of me. There were decisions to be made that affected a lot of people I loved. What a rocky road!

So I asked Him to help me to "go on the heights", just as He had told me to.

Hind's feet Lord, give me hind's feet!
Like yours!

You are the Hind of the morning,
Walk with me on the heights,
Help me to jump, to leap over the crevasses.
You go first – show me how.
Land me safely on sure ground.

Give me a high view of Scripture,
Of the purposes and promises of God.

Grant me a vision from the heights of worship
Of the whole panorama of your will;
And preserve me from the mountain lion
That would terrorize me.
Give me fleet feet when the lion comes.

Yet and though he pounce and bring me down
Help me to bear it well…

And meet me on the other side of sorrow,
In a new place,
    In a new race,
        In a new age,
            On a new page
                Of eternal history.

Until then, oh Heavenly Hind of the morning,
Talk to me often about the dawn of that new day!

Toughen me now, tenderly,
And give me – *Hind's feet*!

By now I had returned through the mists by the way of the valley
to the door of my new day. The phone was ringing off the hook.
The climb had begun. I was ready!

Why not borrow my prayer

for yourself today?

Add some petitions for your

loved ones, too. We,

and they, all need "Hind's

feet"!

ONCE ROUND JERICHO

"THE LORD SAID TO JOSHUA, "SEE, I HAVE DELIVERED JERICHO
INTO YOUR HANDS… MARCH AROUND THE CITY ONCE…"
Joshua 6:2–3

ᘒᕲ

WHY DO I WORRY SO MUCH? Looking back on nearly 70 years of worrying (my mother tells me I was a worried baby!), I am ashamed at my much worrying. Shouldn't being a Christian deal with all of that? I can understand worrying before I knew Jesus, but after I came to know Him as my Saviour? Isn't He supposed to stop all that stress and anxiety that causes me to be an obsessive worrier?

Do you worry about things? Big things and small things; bad things and good things?

I have to say I have won many worry wars, but I have lost nearly as many as I have won! How many times I have run to the Deep Place where nobody goes to talk about it all. I remember once…

"Here I am, Lord, worried again!"

"Yes."

"Do you ever get fed up with me worrying about the same thing over and over and over?"

"I worry about you worrying."

"Yes, I suppose so."

"What is it this time?"

"The same thing as last time!"

"But we talked about it and you seemed to get it all sorted out."

"That was yesterday!"

"It's all the same to me. I saw you last night tossing and turning in bed."

"I know, and I have a huge day ahead of me."

"Worrying empties today of its strength."

"I know."

We were quiet. I felt miserable. Why did I do it? I have tried to come to the Deep Place where nobody goes and give it to Him so many times, but I find whatever the worry of the day is it won't go away. It's like Velcro – somehow stuck to my soul!

I was desperate. "What do I do about this, Lord?"

"Well, if you try to give it to me and it won't go, then give me permission to take it, then go home and forget it."

"Oh."

I thought about that. Well, if I couldn't make it go I could at least give Him permission to unstick the worry from my soul and take it away! I looked at Him. He was looking at me. "Look in my Book," He said. "I have a word for you today."

But I didn't have time just then, as I had to go and give a Bible study on faith and I was running late! So I said with not

too much grace, "I've done this sort of thing so many times, Lord, why should this day be any different?"

He didn't answer, so I just took a quick moment and whispered, "I can't make it go, so I give you permission to take it." I was very still, waiting for I didn't know what. Nothing happened, so I sighed, said goodbye and went out into my busy day.

When I got back from the Deep Place where nobody goes, and walked around the shallow place where everyone lives, I found the reason, for the worry of the day was still there. Nothing had changed. It looked like a huge and formidable "Jericho"! The situation was just as difficult as before, in fact it appeared to have worsened since I began to talk to Him about it.

I don't think I can stop worrying until He makes this mess right, I thought. Ah, now, there was the crux of the problem! What would I do if the problem was never resolved? Worry away until the day I died? Or could there be a hope born in my heart that even if the problem was never solved in my lifetime, I could get to the point of being at peace, believing one day God would answer my worries about this particular thing in His time and in His way?

In other words, could I live with the thing that was causing deep legitimate concern without the wear and tear of obsessive worry about it? I didn't know. All I knew was I was heart sick with worry and I didn't know how to stop! Did I stop praying about it? And what about all the things I was doing with my life? Did I give up ministry till I had "victory"?

The first thing I had to do that day was to teach this Bible lesson on faith to my women's group. "Great," I muttered to the Lord who suddenly appeared and was walking around with me in the shallow places where everyone lives.

I made my way to church and noticed He was sitting in the back row. "Great!" I thought again. I was teaching through the book of Joshua and was up to the battle of Jericho. As I took a deep breath and began, I found myself listening to my own teaching! As I taught the lesson that morning the most amazing thing began to happen. All sorts of new thoughts flooded into my mind.

"Ladies," I said. "The children of Israel were told to go once round Jericho every day and then return to camp and rest until the next day. Round and round they went, once every day for seven days. Then the last day they were told to go round seven times – and the walls fell down. You know," I said (and this is where the new thoughts lined up in my mind like a orderly line of soldiers about to attack the enemy), "it's like worrying. Do you have a Jericho in your life? Are you facing insurmountable problems? I am. I have a terrible situation that is causing me great anxiety." Heads nodded with quiet understanding.

Then I was suddenly aware of His presence. I glanced to the back row, but He was gone. He was, instead, right there in my heart, in my mind, in my spirit – closer than breathing, nearer than hands and feet!

I realized that this was the information he had promised me from His Book. I had been too busy worrying to read it that morning before I set out to teach! I began to get very excited!

"What I do when I am worrying about a Jericho in my life, ladies," I continued, "is this. I wake up with the battle on my mind and begin going round and round, round and round the problem – all day long. I pray about it, but can't stop my mind marching around that impossible situation. I am exhausted at the end of the day! You know God told the children of Israel, who must have been exceedingly worried about their Jericho challenge, to go around the problem *once*, then go back to camp and get on with life till the next day."

I got it! So did they. There was almost a collective sigh of relief in the room.

"Once round Jericho, ladies," I said firmly, as much to myself as to them. You are allowed to wake up and march once around your problem, worrying as much as you like – once! Then you are forbidden to worry any more till the next day. Once round Jericho!"

I couldn't wait to go home and run to the Deep Place where nobody goes. When I got there He was standing by the ruins of something – I realized with a shock it was my Jericho of worry! I began to rehearse a new worry that had appeared on the horizon a day or two before, but He stopped me with a look.

"You have been round this already, looking at it from every angle, Jill" He said sternly. "Now, let's get on with talking about the other people in the camp that have been somewhat ignored because you have been so absorbed." I looked around at the ruins and knew that if I could obey Him, the ruins of my worrying would soon lie around my feet as surely as Jericho crumbled around the feet of the children of Israel. Worry after all is the biggest Jericho of all!

There would be other battles, of course. The children of Israel no sooner got through the problem of Jericho when they were faced with Ai. Another formidable problem around the corner of their victory at Jericho. But the principle would pertain. Once round Jericho!

"Thank you Lord," I almost shouted, "Thank you! Now what about Ai?"

***

Lord, I am weary beyond measure from marching round

each Jericho in my life. Help me to pray my way around the

situation once each day, then leave it with you.

Amen

***

"After all," I thought, as I shut my eyes that night, "the battle is the Lord's".

PRISON LETTERS

"I WAS SICK AND IN PRISON
AND YOU DID NOT VISIT ME."
(Matthew 25:43, RSV)

༄

STUART AND I WERE IN RUSSIA, training Christian leaders from the Caucasus, where some of the churches they are planting are the first in the country. I knew these leaders were going back to places where Christ had not yet been named – where to profess Him was dangerous and only a handful of believers had come to faith.

As Stuart and I were teaching, the men and women in front of us listened with great attention. I was teaching the book of Philippians. We marvelled together how anyone could write the words: "Rejoice in the Lord always. I will say it again, rejoice… be anxious for nothing… and the peace of God will garrison your heart." Paul adds, "I have learned in whatsoever state I am to be content." And this was *from prison*!

At the end of my teaching time the Russians asked me where I would be going in the next few months, so they could pray for me. "Among other things, I'm going to prison in Gatesville, Texas," I said. "There are 11,000 prisoners in the middle of this state, and a friend who works in chaplaincy has invited me to spend a week in three of those facilities: teaching in chapel, going cell to cell, and encouraging the volunteers from churches who minister there."

Three couples came to me at the end of my talk and said: "We work in jails in Dagestan. Some of us, like the prisoners in Gatesville, have been incarcerated not for Christ but for crimes, but we found the Lord in jail. Others of us have been imprisoned for our faith. Now we have a ministry to the men and women in the jails we were in. We want to send a letter to our sisters and brothers in Gatesville, Texas. Will you take it?" I put the precious letter carefully in my Bible.

When I got to the prison in Texas, I felt a little disorientated. Paul was in prison suffering for Christ's sake, while those I mingled with in Texas were suffering as a result of crimes they had committed. Not one was there because they were a Christian. Could I bring the same message to these inmates, from Paul in chains for Christ, as described in the letter to the Philippians, that I had been teaching to church planters in Russia? I decided I could.

What do Dagestan, Russia and Gatesville, Texas have in common? Prisons! Prisons with people in them: lots of people. There are differences, of course. In Dagestan the women who give birth to babies while in jail keep them with them in their cells for three years and then the government takes them away.

Few see them again. In one prison there are over 300 children, I was told.

In Gatesville, Texas, where 11,000 prisoners are housed, there are no children in the cells with their mothers, but I soon learned that the men and women have much in common with the mothers and fathers in Dagestan jails. They desperately miss their kids. The heart hunger is acute. The pain and emotion make it difficult to breathe as they tell you about their children. Oh, the tears!

I read the letter from the Russian believers to each chapel full of prisoners. In some of the chapels we could not talk to the women who were not allowed to stand or sing. In other groups we could stand at the door as they left, to get our arms around them and hug them close, breathing a prayer over each as they lined up to return to their cells.

Many sat still as statues and heard the words of grace and love: words of Paul from prison from the book of Philippians, and the love and promises of prayers from people in Russia half a world away. These were people who had found there is no sin too big for God to forgive. It was as if we had walked into a terminal cancer ward and offered a cure!

I learned that many in this place had come to faith. "It's easy here," the Christian workers told me, "We don't need to convince anyone in Gatesville jail that they're sinners!" I pondered the thought that it was harder to deal with "good sinners" who go to church, than "bad sinners who turn to crime" who don't!

"How good do you have to be to go to heaven?" asked an inmate?

"Perfect!" I replied.

"Then who can go?"

"Only those imperfect people (which includes the whole human race) who have been forgiven their imperfection."

"And how do you get a pardon like that?"

How indeed!

What joy to tell them the story of Barabbas and how he was a sinner caught, tried condemned, and sentenced to death for murder and insurrection. I painted the picture of the guards coming and opening his cell door and telling him he was a free man. (I saw the wondering comprehension in the eyes in front of me!) As Barabbas was caught up in the mob on the way to Calvary, he followed and found his cross there, fully occupied.

I imagined out loud what might have happened. I pictured Barabbas asking John, who seemed to know the man on his cross, who the stranger was. Just who had taken his place? John explained that this was a man called Jesus. He who had healed lepers, opened the eyes of the blind and loved the world that hated Him. He had said He was the Saviour of the world, come to save humankind from the eternal consequences of their sin by being their substitute. Barabbas, I told them, looked at Jesus on the middle cross and simply said: "He's there instead of me! He's taking my place and punishment!"

Some of the women listening intently "got it" and prayed

with me. Others cursed the volunteers out, decided to take their chances with a Holy God, and chose to drown in their hatred and hardness of heart.

In chapel after chapel I had the privilege of standing before hundreds of women in prison garb – in the maximum security block, with death row cells in plain view, or in the reception facility, with frightened wide-eyed newcomers being processed. These women had just been given their number. From now on this would be their identity. Some looked, heartbreakingly, as young as my seven teenage grandchildren. I read the letter from the Russian believers and talked about Paul and the peace of God that passes understanding. I explained that the peace "of" God is only possible when you have been reconciled and have peace "with" God. They cried. I cried. God cried!

The women who were allowed to interact with us were moved mostly by three things.

First, they had never heard about the persecuted church before. They could not believe that people would risk a life sentence in jail for being a Christian. To voluntarily risk jail or worse for Jesus because He went to death row and was executed for crimes He didn't commit – their crimes – blew them away!

The second thing they wanted to talk about were the children in prison. It overwhelmed them to think of having babies in prison, keeping them for three years, and then to have them taken away. Tears flowed again as I read from the Russian letter: "We are trying to have a home for these children in the

Russian prison till the mother is released, so there may be reconciliation. It's hard going though, with much opposition. Please pray for us."

The third thing that made a deep impact was a story I told about meetings I had taken a few years back in a country where Christians were being persecuted.

Thirty-six women huddled in an attic for five days for the first Bible teaching they had ever received. Bibles were not allowed in that land. They had made their way to the upper room willing to turn up at the possible cost of their freedom or even life itself. We taught from eight in the morning to six at night for five days straight. And this without notes! They begged us to teach after supper too! The third day I asked them, "Do you want to worship? I would love to hear you sing one of your hymns." There were excited murmurs among them and my sweet young interpreter said: "Oh that would be wonderful."

I waited. They sang, and the hair went up on the back of my neck. They sang in a whisper! My partner and I listened greatly moved, and I vowed I would never sing loudly and lustily in church again without praying for my sisters in that attic who could only whisper in case they would be discovered.

At that point I had absolutely *no* idea why I was led to share that story with the inmates of Gatesville prison.

The next day some volunteers ate with the inmates. Silence was the rule. This was a surprise, as we didn't know the women were forbidden to talk in many of these venues. Some inmates were on duty in the kitchen. Our team members took their plates and walked to the kitchen hatch with them under the watchful eyes of the strict guards.

They caught their breath as from the inmates who were washing up came the whisper of a familiar melody: "This little light of mine, I'm going to let it shine…"

The women, forbidden to talk, were singing in a whisper! It was a whisper of grace, barely heard. Their watchful eyes widened as a guard suddenly appeared and caught the almost silent worship. The women stopped, nervous and fearful of the guard, and the atmosphere became electric. The guard paused, and then unbelievably joined in like tones: "Let it shine, let it shine, let it shine!" Unheard of! The Jesus lovers in the kitchen took up the whispered words as they – given permission – completed their song and task.

In a few months I would be returning to that attic room in

a country half way round the globe. You can be sure I would take with me the thanks of some sisters, new in Christ, in Gatesville prison who thanks to them have found a way to worship which had been hitherto forbidden!

Sitting quietly in a room in California as I wrote this, I paused to cry again. I had to run to the Deep Place where nobody goes and sit on the steps of my soul. Then I heard His voice as He came close and sat with me. I looked at Him. There was something I didn't quite understand – something to do with his clothes

"Thank you for visiting me, Jill!"

"I am ashamed, Lord. It's only taken me – how many years? Help me make up for lost time!" We sat quietly then and I thought about the faces in Gatesville.

"I miss them all already, Lord – especially the 16-year-old that looks so like our granddaughter, and that frightened little squirrel who doesn't know what to do with herself for the next 17 years."

"I was in prison and you visited me," He said quietly. "Come again."

Then I realized why He looked different. He was wearing prison clothes.

SILENCE

QUIET ME

"Quiet me with your love."
Zephaniah 3:17

———————— ⟋⟍ ————————

ᴀᴠᴇ ʏᴏᴜ ᴇᴠᴇʀ ꜰᴇʟᴛ so assaulted by noise you wanted
to add one more to the cacophony of sound: a scream? They say
an effective torture is constant, super-loud music day and night.

I escaped to a garden seeking respite. I remembered my
mother's love of roses and the plaque she had hanging in her
house. "One is nearer God's heart in a garden than anywhere else
on earth." Sitting in the shade I found it the entrance to the Deep
Place. A shadow shafted with sunbeams drew near. My heart
quieted.

"There are so many voices in the shallow places where
everyone lives," I complained.

"That's why you need to come here more often," He replied.

"Like, more than I do now?"

"Oh yes – a lot more than you do now. You need to live here

and visit the shallow places instead of living in the shallow places and visiting here!"

"Oh, I suppose." Then eagerly: "Quiet me, Lord, quiet me. There's so much noise and discord in my head – my heart can't hear you. Quiet me, Lord – with your love."

I noticed then that in the Deep Places where nobody goes the silence sounds like incredible music from another world – which, of course, I suppose it could be! I listened with that inner ear given to God lovers by the Spirit.

It sounded to me as if all my favourite hymns and songs in the world were all being sung! Can silence sing? Yes, strange as it seems! The silence of God! But how can I describe such silent songs?

Stranger still, as I listened all the songs seemed to be playing at once, and yet I could hear each tune apart and differently. The songs were love songs and oh, oh, oh, He was singing them! I didn't want Him ever to stop. I found myself responding: "Quiet me – with your love."

"Love is quietness," He reminded me later, as I reluctantly prepared to leave the garden of grace. "Stay long enough, Jill, to gather a soul full of quietude to bless your noisy world!" I did. I knew the people in the shallow places were waiting.

Find a garden. When you're sitting in the

Spirit's shade, pray: "Quiet me, Lord: quiet me

with your love." Then listen to the silence sing.

Jill Briscoe and her husband Stuart live in
Milwaukee, Wisconsin. They have worked
together for over 40 years, and have three
grown children and thirteen grandchildren.
A native of Liverpool, Jill is a prolific writer.
She serves on the board of directors of
World Relief and of *Christianity Today*, and is
a popular speaker at key Christian events
around the world.